Praise for *Pay Me*

"Pay Me *is a clear, practical guide for young people venturing for the first time into the world of paid employment. It explains in down-to-earth terms how getting a job – and getting paid – actually works. This is the essential, jargon-free guide every parent/guardian should have to hand when helping their child navigate the maze of landing their first job and understanding what happens once they start earning. A genuinely useful book, and one that fills a long-standing gap.*"

Cathy Higginson, mother of two boys

"*I started reading this book and, within a few pages, I felt I could see where Hayley was taking me, so I wrote my review then and decided to revisit it once I had finished reading to see if anything had changed in my views, which it hadn't. Hayley has demonstrated that you do not need to, nor should you, rely solely on your employer to determine what your financial future will look like. There are no big secrets to earning money, just a lot of small but important steps, and Hayley has concisely provided these in an easy-to-follow format, which should be continuously referred to throughout your working/earning life. I wish I had read this 25 years ago! I was fortunate that my parents shared their knowledge with me, and I asked other people questions, but having all of the information in this book to hand back when I was first starting to earn some money would have certainly helped me along the way. Do not underestimate the power of compound interest on your pensions and investments, regardless of how early/small you start.*"

Gareth Vaughan, father of a boy and a girl

"Pay Me *is a useful guide for young people entering the world of work and managing money for the first time. The book provides relatable analogies and breaks down complex topics in a way that is easy to understand. It's the kind of book I wish I had access to before joining the workforce."*

Corinna Patience, Teacher – Business Studies

"Amazing book. It's helpful but also fun to read. I learnt much more than I thought and will definitely read it again when I'm older."

Chloe Mudge, aged 13

"I found this book contains a lot of useful things about payslips, CVs, pensions and a lot more. Overall, I think this book will be very useful for people to learn about pay and how it works."

Fred Mudge, aged 15

"I found this book very useful, as a young adult who has been working from a young age."

Julia Sutor, aged 17

"As someone who is in the target age bracket for this book, I found it very helpful. Absolutely a useful tool for all young people looking to get their first job, work their way up the job ladder, or even learn some great budgeting strategies. The book covers all these topics and more. A comprehensive guide, while being clear and concise. Highly recommend."

Connor Fraser, aged 18

"As someone with very minimal knowledge of payroll, I found this book to be a great starting point for learning and getting more involved. I was pleasantly surprised by how different, informative and relaxed it felt. I really enjoyed how friendly the writing was and how it made the whole idea of payroll feel approachable, rather than just a load of complicated numbers. This book would be incredibly useful for anyone looking for employment, for those who are struggling to find work, or to understand the best way to go about gaining employment."

Kelly Morrison, aged 20

"I think this book could be very useful. It's the kind of resource I would have benefited from when I was first starting out in the world of work. In particular, the career pathways and strategy section feels especially valuable; a practical guide for young people early in their careers (around 16–18), helping them plan ahead and prepare the ground early."

Fergus Maxwell, aged 23

PAY ME

YOUR GUIDE TO ENTERING THE WORLD OF WORK WITH CONFIDENCE AND DIRECTION

HAYLEY PATERSON

Cover image by: Blunt Design, 99D
Book design by: SWATT Books Ltd
Editing and proofreading by: Craig Smith (CRS Editorial)

Printed in the United Kingdom
First Printing, 2026

ISBN: 978-1-0684476-2-4 (Paperback)
ISBN: 978-1-0684476-3-1 (eBook)

Hayley Paterson
Fortrose Scotland

www.thepayrollguide.co.uk

Contents

To my husband, Michael:

Thank you for standing beside me through every chapter, for your unwavering support, and for being the most loving, amazing father to our son. You are forever my anchor. I couldn't have written this without you.

To my son, Alfie:

You inspire me daily with the person you're growing into. You are my reason and my pride. This book was written with you in mind, to guide and support you when you're ready to step into the world of work. Thank you for your motivational chats, which kept me going.

To my nephew, Fred, and my nieces, Chloe and Beth:

This book is for you too, as you set out on your life adventures. I'm forever your personal access to payroll knowledge.

To my early readers, especially the academy pupils who peer-reviewed this book and impressed me with their thoughtful insights; to my book mentor, Karen; my editor, Craig; my publishing consultant, Sam; and all those who shared feedback and support on LinkedIn... you inspire me, you teach me, and I thank you.

Prologue

The world of work looks enormous from your eyes, like a city skyline you're seeing for the first time. You know it's full of possibilities, but it's also a little intimidating. Everyone talks about 'careers' and 'the future' like you're supposed to have it all figured out, when half the time, you're still trying to decide what you want for lunch.

At first, work feels like something older people do – people with briefcases, meetings and mysterious calendars full of colour-coded chaos. But then you take your first step into it: maybe a weekend job, a summer shift, or an office junior role, where you wear shoes that feel slightly too formal. Suddenly, the abstract becomes real. You notice how good it feels to earn your own money, and how empowering it is to know you made that happen.

There's excitement...your first payslip, your first 'Well done', and your first moment of thinking, 'I can actually do this'. There's fear too. What if I'm not good enough? What if I choose the wrong path? But underneath those worries is something stronger – curiosity. A tug that says, 'What else could I be?'.

As you move through each new experience, the world of employment starts to look less like a maze and more like a map. Every job teaches you something about yourself, what you enjoy, what drains you, and what sparks that quiet ambition you didn't realise was sitting inside you.

Bit by bit, dreams stop feeling like 'one day' ideas and start feeling like plans. Maybe you'll run something, build something, lead something. Maybe you'll create change that matters.

The truth is...employment isn't just about earning. It's about discovering who you are becoming, and realising that the future isn't waiting for the 'right time'. It's unfolding now, one bold step at a time.

It's your employment journey, so take the steering wheel.

You decide the direction, the pace, and when it's time to change course. Within these pages is your Google Map, helping you understand the route ahead, spot potential roadblocks, and choose the best path for where you want to go. You're still the driver, but with the right guidance, you're less likely to take a wrong turn or end up lost.

Remember, it's not just about the destination. It's as much about the journey, and what you learn, build and become along the way.

Let's Get to Work

Your practical guide to the process of getting paid, and the strategy to keep your income growing.

LET'S BE HONEST, money is the biggest reason we go to work. You trade your time, your energy and your skills, and in return, you get paid. Simple, right? At least, that's what I thought when I first started out. You work; they pay. End of story.

But getting paid has more moving parts than most people realise. If you don't understand them, you can quickly find yourself underpaid, overlooked, or confused.

Maybe you're filling in your first job application and have no idea how to present yourself in the best way. Maybe you've just landed a weekend or after-school job and stared at your first payslip, wondering what it all means. Maybe your rota changed at the last minute, your hours didn't add up, and you weren't sure what to do. Maybe you accepted a job because the pay sounded good, until you realised what hit your bank account. Or maybe you've been grafting hard, hoping someone will notice, but don't really know how people 'move up'.

If any of that sounds familiar, you're not alone. Most people at the start of their working lives feel unsure, under-informed, and a bit lost in the noise. I know, because I've lived it. And that's exactly what this book is here to fix.

This book is for you if you're just starting out...whether that's your first weekend or summer job, or you're leaving school or college and stepping into the world of work.

If you're finishing university, there can be a bit more to navigate, as graduate roles often come with more specific requirements and expectations. You'll still get a lot from this book – it provides a strong foundation in how the worlds of work and pay operate – but you'll also want to lean on your university's careers service for more specialised, technical guidance in your chosen field.

I started my employment journey at a young age, babysitting, cleaning holiday cottages and giving horse-riding lessons. Just doing whatever came my way. At 16, I went to college to study equine management, but that path fizzled out.

From there, I waited tables, worked in shops, a call centre, and handled admin jobs. Then redundancy struck, and led me to payroll, a role I was unqualified for and never planned on. But it ended up being a profession I fell in love with.

My employment path has been anything but a straight line. I've spent over two decades working in payroll, across industries, the oil and gas sector, and several payroll bureaux for companies, big and small. I now run two payroll businesses: Chanonry Payroll Solutions (outsource provider) and The Payroll Guide (payroll consulting).

This means I've been on all sides of the payslip. I've been the person waiting for payday, the person providing the payslips for businesses, and the employer providing them to my own team.

Along the way, I've seen it all. Confused employees who didn't know why their pay was lower than expected, managers baffled by pay periods, and young people who thought pensions were something to worry about later in life.

The thing is, payroll isn't just about numbers. It's about you, your rights, your choices, and your future.

Every odd job, every twist and turn, taught me something I'd later need. There's no such thing as a wrong path, just your unique adventure. What I thought were wrong turns, ended up being my greatest lessons, providing the knowledge and experience that serve me today.

If I could go back and talk to my younger self, fresh into my first job, there are so many things I'd speak about:

- How to read a payslip without my eyes glazing over
- Why contracts aren't scary, but a map of my rights
- What 'competitive salary' means in a job ad
- Why pensions are more money for no more work (and why future me would thank myself for caring, early)
- How to speak up if something goes wrong with my pay
- What to do with what hits my bank account.

Nobody explained those things to me. I had to figure them out the hard way. That's why I wrote *Pay Me*.

This book is for young people, like you, who want to start their working lives with confidence instead of confusion, whether you're stepping into your first job or your fifth. If you've ever stared at your payslip feeling lost, questioned your rights, or wondered how to turn payday into more than just money hitting your account, you're in the right place. *Pay Me* is your guide to understanding how pay really works, avoiding the traps that hold people back, and building a career with purpose, clarity and momentum...under your control.

I promise this isn't a dry textbook or a pile of jargon. It's a practical guide for understanding how pay really works, written in plain language, with insights I've collected over the years.

Knowing how pay works doesn't mean you just get paid right. It means you can plan, grow and make choices with your eyes wide open. Pay isn't the end goal; it's the foundation for building the life you want.

Welcome to *Pay Me*.

How This Book Works

I've split this book into two parts, because getting paid isn't just about understanding the system. It's about using it to your advantage, with strategy.

Part 1: The Process

Think of this part as lifting the lid on payroll. It will take you step by step from looking for a job to money landing in your bank account. I'll break down how pay works, from job adverts, interviews and contracts, to payslips, tax, pensions, and what to do if things go wrong. Once you understand this, you'll never look at payday the same again.

Part 2: The Strategy

Before you can build the future you want, you need to spot the opportunities sitting right in front of you. Your payslip isn't just proof you got paid, it's the starting point for earning smarter and growing faster. Here you'll learn to work with purpose using my Skills Collector Roadmap to build the abilities that raise your value, and my Connection Builder Framework to create relationships that open real opportunities. When you understand the game, and that not all jobs, shifts or skills pay the same, you will stop drifting and start making strategic moves that shape your future.

Pro Tips and Downloads

As you read through the book, I'll drop in pro tips to highlight quick wins, smart shortcuts, and things you shouldn't overlook.

You'll also get downloadable templates that turn the ideas in this book into action steps you can take today.

Extra Help at the End

To make everything in this book even easier to use, I've added two powerful sections at the end:

- **Jargon Buster:** A quick, plain-language guide to all the payroll terms you'll come across. No more scratching your head at 'National Insurance contributions' or 'Gross vs Net'.
- **Handy Links:** Resources, websites and tools you can use if you want to dive deeper, check your rights, or get extra help.

Whether you've mapped out your dream job or you're still figuring things out, *Pay Me* gives you the tools and confidence to understand your pay, own your worth, and take charge of the future you want.

PART 1:
The Process

Getting paid isn't magic,
it's a process.

BEFORE YOU CAN earn well or negotiate confidently, you need to understand the world you're stepping into. Not in a boring, bureaucratic way, but in a 'this is your money and your future' kind of way. The system isn't complicated on purpose. It's just never been explained to you in a way that makes sense.

Part 1 gives you the real-world foundations of getting paid, which you're rarely taught, but life expects you to know anyway. It's where you learn how pay is shaped, how rules protect you, and how to spot when something doesn't look right.

From CVs that tell your real story, to job adverts that aren't always as shiny as they seem. From interviews where you prove your worth, to contracts that spell out your rights. From the hours you work, to the pay you take home, and the payslips that quietly tell the truth. This is the backbone of your working life.

Once you understand it, you will stop drifting through jobs and will start to purposely steer your way through your employment journey. You will stop accepting whatever you're given and start claiming what you've earned. You will become the kind of person who knows how the system works and knows how to work it for yourself.

So, let's break down the process, step by step. It will become clear, practical and empowering. Exactly what you need to build confidence, avoid mistakes and take control of your pay from day one.

CHAPTER 1

CV: How to Get Noticed

Before they meet you,
they meet your CV.

IF YOU WANT to land a job, whether it's a weekend/summer gig, a part-time role, or your first big step into the working world, you need a CV that quickly shows employers why you deserve a place on their interview shortlist.

You've probably heard the term 'CV' (curriculum vitae) thrown around a hundred times, but what actually is it, and why does everyone make such a fuss about it? In this chapter, I'll break it down, show you what really matters and make sure you know how to use your CV as a tool not just a document.

The good news? You don't need loads of experience to create a standout CV. Even if you're just starting out, have only had one or two jobs, or only have school or work-experience placements to talk about, and even if you're not great at bigging yourself up, you've still got more to offer than you realise. I'll show you how to turn what you do have into a strong CV that gets you one step closer to that payslip.

But before I dive into creating a high-impact CV, let's take a step back and figure out what pay you're looking for. If this is your first weekend/summer job, it might be a little early for this, but it'll help you plan for the future.

You need to be clear on the wages you need to live on. If the wages an employer offers can't realistically cover your basic requirements, the job won't work for you in the long run, no matter how great it looks on paper. Knowing your minimum number helps you apply smarter, negotiate with confidence, and avoid ending up in a role that leaves you stressed before payday even arrives.

Exercise: Calculate Your 'Must-have' Number

Grab a pen or your phone and list everything you need to pay for each month. Examples might include travel, food, bills, phone, subscriptions, and anything else you're responsible for. Include a monthly allowance for things like new clothes, household items, new car etc. If you're still at home with your parents/guardians, then add in what you'd need if you were living in your own place. This will help you become independent, faster.

Decide how much you'd like to put away for savings each month (start small and build on it when you're able to). Then add a realistic amount for enjoying life: seeing friends, hobbies, the little things that make your weeks feel good. Add it all together. That total is your minimum pay requirement for a month – the baseline you should keep in mind when looking at any job.

Note: The pay in a job advert is not what you'll end up with in your bank. There are statutory deductions to come off (more on these in Chapters 6, 7 and 9). For now, calculate the amount you need in the bank (net pay).

Your 'must-have' number will develop over time. You may not even know what it is when you're looking for your first job. I recommend revisiting this exercise regularly, and developing your ideal number now, in one year, in five years, and perhaps your dream number. Mapping out where you want to go helps you get there, and faster.

Download:

Want help figuring out your employment must-haves? Visit www.thepayrollguide.co.uk/pay-me and grab the spreadsheet I've put together to help guide you.

Now you've got a clearer idea of how much money you need, it's time to create your CV and get the job that can deliver it.

If you want to land that job, you need to show employers why they should pick you out of all the other applicants.

But don't worry, as I said before, you don't need a wide array of experience to create a CV that shines. Let's get started with the basics.

What Exactly Is a CV?

A CV is like your personal highlights reel. It's a carefully chosen snapshot of your best moments so far – the skills you've built, the experiences you've had (even if that's helping out at your uncle's bakery for a few hours on a Saturday), and the strengths you bring. Its job is to help employers quickly understand who you are, what you can do, and why you're worth inviting to an interview, without needing every detail of your story. Get it right, and it's your ticket to getting noticed and, ultimately, getting paid.

First Things First: What Do Employers Care About?

Before you start writing anything, you've got to understand what employers want to see. Here's a little secret: they're not expecting you to have 10 years of experience at 16 or 24 years of age. What they care about is your potential, your attitude to work, and what you can bring to the table. If you want to get paid well, you've got to show you're worth their investment.

Think about it like this: employers are willing to give you their money in exchange for your time, skills and effort. Your CV needs to make them feel confident that hiring you is a smart decision. That means you've got to present your best self, not just who you are right now, but also who you're working to become.

The Structure of a CV: The Building Blocks

Your typed CV isn't a free-for-all. It needs structure. Think of it like building a house – you need a solid foundation, clear rooms (or sections), and some personal touches to make it stand out.

Here's how to break it down:

Contact Information

Start with the basics:

- Full name
- Email address (make sure it's professional; maybe not the one you created when you were 12 with 'unicornlover67' in it)
- Mobile number
- Location.

This part should be clean and easy to read. If they can't contact you, they can't invite you to an interview!

Personal Profile/Objective

This is where you briefly introduce yourself. Think of it as your elevator pitch (a short and sweet introduction).

Example:
'Motivated high-school graduate with a passion for technology and problem-solving, seeking a part-time position in customer service. Eager to contribute to a team environment while gaining experience in the workplace.'

This should always be tailored to each job you apply for, making sure it aligns with the job description/specification they've provided.

Here are some quick tips on how to write an effective personal profile, without sounding like you're showing off:

- Write it for the employer not for yourself – Focus on the value you bring and not how great you are. Think about the problem that you help solve.
- Be specific not grand – Swap vague claims like 'results-driven' for clear facts, skills or outcomes.
- Keep it short – 2-4 lines is plenty. If it's any longer, it usually drifts into waffle.
- Use plain language – If you wouldn't say it out loud, don't write it. Simple beats trying to sound impressive, every time.
- Show direction – Mention what you're aiming for or interested in – it shows purpose without bragging.
- Let evidence do the talking – Hint at experience or results, then prove it in the rest of your CV.
- Avoid buzzwords and clichés – If it appears on hundreds of CVs, it won't help yours stand out.

- A rule of thumb is – If it sounds like you're trying to impress, rewrite it so it sounds like you're trying to be useful.

You can use tools like ChatGPT to help shape what you want to say, smoothing the flow or adjusting the tone. But it still needs to sound like you. Always read through what's produced and tweak it, so your own voice shines through.

Watch out for words you'd never use in real conversation. Big, fancy wording might look impressive on paper, but if it's not natural to you, it can come across as insincere, and that's a quick way to lose trust.

List of Key Skills

Listing your key skills at the top of your CV is a smart move because it quickly shows an employer what you bring to the table. Recruiters often scan CVs in seconds, so putting your most relevant skills front and centre helps them instantly see why you're a good fit. It also sets the tone for the rest of your CV, giving context to your experience and making it easier to connect the dots between what you can do and what the role needs. Again, tailor the skills you list to the requirements of the job you're applying for.

Education

Whether you're still in school, recently graduated, or taking a gap year, your education matters. List where you're studying or studied, your expected (or actual) graduation date, the grades you've achieved, and any relevant coursework or academic achievements. Don't worry if you're not top of the class, just be honest and put your best foot forward.

Work Experience

Here's where a lot of people freak out, because they think they don't have enough to list. If this is your first job, relax – work experience isn't just about 'real' jobs with payslips. Babysitting your neighbour's children? That counts. Helping your friend with their YouTube channel? Yep, that too. Tutoring your little brother? You've got it.

For each job or experience you've had, list:

- The position you held
- The place you worked or volunteered
- The dates (if you're unsure, then approximate dates are fine)
- A couple of bullet points describing what you did and, more importantly, what skills you gained.

Pro Tip:

Tie the skills and experience you've gained in each job to the role you're applying for. It shows you understand what the employer needs and makes it easy for them to see the match. Pick the skills that fit. For example, communication and people skills for customer service; organisation and attention to detail for office roles.

Here's an example:

Summer 2026: Team Member, The Coffee House Ltd

- Served customers
- Managed the register
- Maintained a clean workspace

- Developed communication and time-management skills by balancing tasks during busy hours.

Even if you don't think it's impressive, everything you've done counts, because it all gives you experience.

Skills

You have listed your key skills. Now it's time to show off a little. Here's where you list all the things you're good at. Employers love skills, and even if you haven't worked before, you've definitely got some. Split skills into two categories. Listing your skills in 'hard-skill' and 'soft-skill' categories makes your CV easier to scan and shows what you can do and how you work, helping employers quickly see your full value.

Hard skills include technical skills, like knowing how to use a type of software, speak another language, write code, or operate specific equipment.

Soft skills (also known as transferable or meta-skills) are personal traits, like being a good communicator, time management, staying organised, problem-solving, or being a team player.

Download:
Visit www.thepayrollguide.co.uk/pay-me and download my hard-skills examples and soft-skills list. It'll help you figure out the strengths you already have.

Hobbies and Interests

This section might seem optional, but it can help give employers a better sense of who you are. It's especially helpful if you don't have much work experience. If you're really into sports, music, or any extracurricular activities, list them! They can show that you're well-rounded, committed and enthusiastic. They help highlight transferable skills and help employers see how you'll fit in with their existing team.

Just be mindful of what you list. It's probably not a good idea to mention how much time you spend binge-watching Netflix, YouTube, or the hours you spend gaming. But time spent playing in a football team shows teamwork and commitment.

References

References are people who can vouch for you, like a teacher, coach, or former employer. If you've never worked before, no worries, a mentor or family friend who knows you well can still give a character reference. You don't need to include their full details right away; just write 'Available upon request'. Make sure you have the permission of the people you have given as references, before giving out their contact details.

There are a few things you want to avoid putting on your CV. These are:

- Age and date of birth – Including this information can lead to age bias.
- Full address – Your city and country of residence are sufficient. Listing your full address is unnecessary and

can raise security concerns or lead to assumptions about commute times.

- Marital status and family information – Details such as whether you're single, married or have children are irrelevant to your professional capabilities and are protected characteristics.
- Gender, sexual orientation, race or religion – Any information that indicates these characteristics should be left out as it can lead to discrimination.
- Nationality – This is unnecessary and can be omitted at this stage. Your eligibility to work in the UK is something that will need to be verified later in the hiring process, if you're successful.
- Disability or health information – You are not required to disclose health information or any disability at the application stage, unless you need reasonable adjustments for the interview process itself.
- A photo of you – Photos can open up the possibility of unconscious bias (when assumptions affect decisions without people realising it) based on appearance.

This might seem strange, but by creating an anonymised CV, you help ensure that employers evaluate you solely on your professional merits, skills and qualifications.

Tailoring Your CV for the Job You Want

Your CV isn't a one-size-fits-all document, but what does this mean? Every job you apply for is different, so you need to tweak your CV for each position. Don't worry, this doesn't mean starting from scratch every time, but you do want to highlight different skills or experiences based on the job description. This can be as simple as looking for key words, and mirroring them in your CV and covering letter. This shows you've paid attention to what the employer requires, and allows you to clearly demonstrate how you have what they need, or if you don't yet, how you're working on obtaining these skills.

The Covering Letter

Including a covering letter with your CV is a smart move because it gives you the chance to show personality, motivation and context – things a CV alone cannot fully capture. It lets you explain why you want the role, highlight your most relevant strengths, and connect your experience directly to what the employer is looking for. Keep it short and focused, tailor it to each job, and avoid repeating your CV word-for-word. Write in a clear, confident voice, show genuine interest in the company, and always finish with a polite, proactive closing.

The Secret to Getting Paid: Your CV is Step One

To get paid, you need a job. To get a job, you need an interview. To get an interview, you need a CV that gets you noticed. Employers want people who add value – someone reliable, capable, coachable and ready to make their lives easier. That's what they're paying for. Your CV needs to prove you're that person.

Your potential boss is looking at your CV thinking, 'Is this person worth paying?'. So, make sure your CV answers that with a confident, 'Yes!'.

Final Tips to Make Your CV Stand Out

Keep it to one or two pages. Seriously. Employers don't have time to read a novel. Be concise and make sure every word counts.

Use action verbs like 'created', 'managed', 'developed' or 'organised' to describe your responsibilities and achievements. It makes your experience sound more impressive.

Check your spelling and grammar, as tiny slip-ups can cost you more than you think. Employers often skim dozens of CVs, and small mistakes can make you look careless, even if you're not. Run your CV through a spellcheck, ask someone you trust to proofread it, or use AI tools (like ChatGPT) to help tighten up your wording and spot anything you've missed. A clean, polished CV shows you've put the effort in...and that counts. As previously mentioned, be wary of using AI too much, as your CV will lose personality and that's what employers want to see. If you do use AI to assist, make sure your CV still sounds like you.

Creating your first CV might seem intimidating, but once you get started, it's just a matter of putting your best self on paper.

Download:
Head over to www.thepayrollguide.co.uk/pay-me for a template to get you started.

Up Next

You've powered up your CV, which is great! But a strong CV only works when you know where to point it. Up next, I'll talk you through job adverts, so you can read between the lines and match what employers want with what you've got.

Takeaways

- Know your number – Before you write your CV, figure out the pay you need to live on, so you only apply for roles that genuinely work for you.
- You don't need loads of experience – A great CV isn't about having tons of jobs, it's about showing your potential, your attitude and the skills you have.
- Structure is everything – A clear layout with contact information, a personal profile, education, work experience, skills, and hobbies and interests, make it easy for employers to spot what matters.
- Everything counts as experience – Babysitting, school projects, work experience placements, helping in family businesses; it all builds skills you can use.
- Tailor every CV and covering letter – A one-size-fits-all CV doesn't work. Highlight the skills and experience that match each job description.

- Keep it sharp and spotless – One to two pages maximum, use action verbs for impact, and make sure there are no spelling mistakes. Your CV should look polished, focused and ready for the shortlist.

CHAPTER 2

Cracking the Job Adverts Code

Job adverts are like dating profiles;
they sound good, but what's the reality?

JOB ADS CAN be sneaky. Businesses often dangle words like 'competitive pay' or 'great benefits' without telling you what they are. This chapter shows you how to read between the lines, so you know what's really on offer before you step through the door.

So, you're ready to dive into the job market. You have an idea of your 'must-have' number (from the previous chapter's exercise) and you've decided what kind of job you're looking for. These are big steps, so congratulations! If you are yet to decide exactly what you want to do, then determine what skills or experiences you want to gain, and think about when, where and how you'd like to work.

Now you need to find that job...but where?

The good news is there are loads of places to start looking:

- Local businesses
- Local community hubs and village halls
- Groups like the Scouts and Brownies will open-up connections to local businesses
- School/university career fairs and employer links
- Word of mouth
- Family or friends' connections
- Newspapers
- LinkedIn
- Facebook community groups
- Online job sites, like Indeed or Glassdoor
- Recruitment agencies
- Government initiatives, like Developing the Young Workforce (DYW) in Scotland – a Scottish Government initiative to better prepare young people for the world of work.

Tap into your connections. For example, who does your family know, who runs a business? Look into tutoring, babysitting, dog walking, or helping out at local events.

Think local. Cafés, shops, gyms, cinemas and supermarkets are often happy to hire younger staff, especially for weekends or evenings. Don't overlook smaller independent businesses either, as they love reliable part-timers.

If you're more digitally minded, online platforms like Indeed and LinkedIn often post flexible roles.

The key is to stay open-minded, ask around, get creative and remember that your first job is more about getting experience and skills than finding your forever career.

Whether you're after a part-time gig to keep you afloat during college or ready to kickstart your dream career, job adverts are where it all starts. If job ads feel like decoding some ancient language, then fear not. By the time you finish this chapter, you'll be ready to sift through them like a pro.

Here are parts of a job advert to look out for:

The Headline: Don't Let It Fool You

Job titles can be misleading. You might see something like 'Helpdesk Technician' or 'Client Service Consultant' which sound cool, right? Fancy titles like these often hide ordinary, customer service roles. It's therefore important to read beyond the headline. Get to the meat of the description before you fall for the catchy phrasing.

The Job Description: Read Between the Lines

Here's where most people speed-read and miss out on key details. Job ads often list tasks, requirements and sometimes a bit about the business' culture. But look closely! If they're asking for someone who is 'able to work in a fast-paced environment', this is code for you will be busy all day, every day. Similarly, 'must be a team player' usually means get ready to collaborate...a lot.

An employer may require hard skills, which are job-specific and often technical (like knowing how to code or operate a specific type of machinery).

They're also likely to want soft skills. As mentioned in the previous chapter, these are your personal attributes, traits and abilities that enable you to interact effectively and harmoniously with others. These skills are crucial for building relationships, solving problems and thriving in almost any job.

Don't panic if they list a bunch of skills you don't have. If you meet 70% of what's required, you should apply! No one's perfect, and many employers are happy to train the right person.

It's worth considering:

- Can you be trained on the technicalities of the role?
- How coachable are you?
- Are you dependable and honest?
- How do you manage your time?

Pro Tip:
Look out for key words in the job description that indicate the soft skills required for the role. Refer back to Chapter 1 for what soft skills are. As an example, if a job description says 'you'll work closely with different teams and communicate clearly with clients', the key soft skills to highlight are communication, teamwork and relationship-building.

Salary: Don't Let 'Competitive' Put You Off

A lot of job ads will list the salary as 'competitive' or 'depending on experience', but what do these terms mean?

Basically, they are fancy ways of saying, 'we're not telling you how much you'll get paid, yet!'.

Don't let this scare you off, but proceed with caution. If you get to the interview stage and the salary is below your expectations, presuming you're offered the job, you can always negotiate or decide to keep looking. The worst-case scenario? You've picked up some great interview experience. You'll likely find jobs that are more transparent about pay. It's okay to ask about salary before you go any further, but if you do bring it up, make it clear that money isn't your only motivator. There's no point wasting your time, or the employer's.

Pro Tip:
Before applying, check websites like Indeed or Glassdoor to see if they have salary information for that business. Also, do an internet search for the average salary in your area for the job you're looking for. It'll give you a rough idea of what to expect. Bear in mind though, you are new to this type of role, and that someone with more experience is likely to get paid more.

The Experience Trap

You see a job advert asking for five years' experience when you've only just left school. Classic.

Lots of employers list things they *want*, rather than things they *actually need*. That's the difference between 'desired' and 'mandatory', and it applies to everything from experience to qualifications. If they say, 'experience with Microsoft Office' and you've used Word for school projects, guess what? You've got experience. Apply.

If you're short on experience, focus on your transferable skills. Have you worked in a team at school? Solved problems for a volunteer project? Managed a club or sports team? You've likely already got teamwork, problem-solving and leadership skills without even realising it.

Pro Tip:
Always be upfront about your experience. If you show a desire to learn, you might convince the employer to take a chance on you.

Full-time vs Part-time: It's a Numbers Game

When it comes to hours, pay close attention to what you're signing up for. Full-time usually means 35-40 hours per week in the UK, but part-time can vary widely. If you're a student or looking for a role with flexibility, part-time work can be ideal. Just make sure the hours align with your availability.

Some job ads might say 'full-time preferred but part-time considered'. This is a great opportunity to negotiate if you need fewer hours.

Pro Tip:
Before you accept a job, make sure you fully understand the type of contract you'll be on, as it can shape your work and your lifestyle. More on contracts in Chapter 4.

The key is to think about what matters most to you right now: security or flexibility? Again, there's no one-size-fits-all, but being aware of the trade-offs will help you choose a contract that supports your goals and lifestyle.

Location, Location, Location

It sounds obvious, but make sure you check where the job's based. Is it in a place you can get to easily? A bigger city might offer a lot of roles, but if you live rurally and don't want to move, commuting isn't exactly going to be fun...or cheap.

If you're applying for jobs in major cities, factor the higher commuting and/or living costs into your pay requirements.

You don't want your pay being swallowed by train fares/rent. Higher costs mean less of your net pay available for saving and for living life.

Pro Tip:
Look out for roles that offer remote or hybrid working, where you can split your time between home and the office. More UK employers are offering this flexibility, but whether it works for you depends on the job and your situation. When you're training, being in the workplace can speed up your learning. If you're living with your parents/guardians, sharing a noisy flat with friends on different shifts, or you're easily distracted, working from home might not be as dreamy as it sounds. Even with flexibility, the work still needs to get done, so choose a setup that helps you focus.

'Must Have a Driving Licence' – Seriously?

Even if you don't drive, don't immediately write off a job that asks for a licence, depending on what it is, of course. Sometimes, businesses throw this requirement in, but it's not always essential. You can ask if it's a dealbreaker before you apply, especially if public transport works well for getting around, or you live close by.

The Small Print

Some job adverts include a bit about qualifications, especially for roles in law, finance, engineering, childcare, or health and safety.

If a job needs a specific qualification or licence, it's usually non-negotiable. This isn't about employers being picky; it's often a legal or professional requirement. Always double-check these sections so you know whether you meet the criteria, or if it's something you could realistically work towards.

Then there are the essentials that every employer must check, like your right to work in the UK. This isn't optional. When you start a job, you'll need to provide proof such as a passport, visa or other approved documentation. Even if the advert only mentions it briefly, it's a key part of the hiring process, so make sure you understand what applies to you and have your documents ready.

Look out for deadlines as well. Some businesses might close applications after a certain number of candidates apply, even if the deadline hasn't passed, so the sooner you apply, the better.

Think of a job advert like a concert or festival ticket. Some events are open to everyone, but others have strict entry rules. If the ticket says 'over 18s only' or 'photo ID required', it's not the organiser being awkward, it's a legal requirement. Turning up without ID or being underage means you won't get in, no matter how enthusiastic you are.

Qualifications, licences and right-to-work checks work the same way. They're your entry pass.

These requirements aren't about preferences; they're about access and timing.

Filling in Applications: Getting Past the First Gate

Once you've found a job advert that sparks your interest, the next step is applying, and this is where many people trip up. Gone are the days of simply handing in a CV at reception. Most employers now use online systems to collect and manage applications.

It might be a case of emailing your CV and covering letter to a specific email address, or you might need to apply through a recruitment portal. This might mean uploading your CV, filling in online forms, answering short questions, or completing questionnaires. Some systems save your progress so you can come back later, but don't rely on this. Always keep a copy of your answers somewhere safe.

Treat every application like it's your first impression, because it is. Check spelling, read questions carefully and don't rush. Many employers use automated systems to scan applications for key words from the job advert, so tailoring your answers matters more than ever.

Job applications aren't just paperwork; they're the first filter. The goal is simple: make it easy for the employer to see that you're worth meeting. Follow instructions, present yourself clearly and don't be put off by the technology. Once you understand the system, you're already ahead of many applicants.

Video Applications and Online Screening

Some employers ask for video applications instead of (or as well as) written ones. You might be asked to record short answers to set questions using your phone or laptop. It can feel awkward at first, but remember, they're not expecting a movie-star performance. Speak clearly, be yourself and keep your answers focused.

You may also come across online screening tests, such as personality questionnaires, basic maths or literacy checks, or situational judgement questions. These aren't designed to catch you out; they help employers understand how you think and work. Take your time, read the instructions carefully and answer honestly.

Dodgy Job Ads: What to Watch Out For

While most job adverts are legit, there are some that are too good to be true. Be wary of:

- Vague descriptions – Tread carefully if the role sounds too vague or an employer is offering way more money than the job seems worth.
- Upfront fees – You should never have to pay for training or equipment upfront. If an employer is asking for money before you've even started, it's likely a scam.
- Personal details – Be cautious about ads that ask for personal information like your National Insurance (NI) number or bank details at the application stage. This is a red flag.

The Next Steps

Found a job you like? Great! Before applying, make sure you tailor your CV, like I mentioned in Chapter 1, to highlight the skills they're asking for. Use keywords from the job description and show them you're the perfect fit. Remember, job hunting is a numbers game.

Recruiters and employers will get many applications, and have busy schedules, so don't get discouraged if you don't hear back from every application. Keep going!

Up Next

You've cracked the job ads and found roles worth going for...nice work! Now it's time to nail the interview. Let's look at what employers really want, and how you can show up confident and prepared.

Takeaways

- Job ads aren't always what they seem – Headlines can be flashy or misleading. Always dig into the details before deciding if a role is right for you.
- Read between the lines – Phrases like 'fast-paced' or 'team player' are clues about the work environment and expectations. Decode them to understand the reality of the job.
- Wording matters – Terms like 'competitive' usually mean the employer isn't revealing pay yet. Do your research, ask early and compare with your 'must-have' number from the Chapter 1 exercise.
- Experience requirements are flexible – 'Five years' experience' often means 'we'd prefer it', not 'you must have it'. If you meet around 70% of the requirements, apply anyway.

- Spot red flags early – Vague job descriptions, requests for upfront payment, or demands for personal details at the application stage can signal a scam. Trust your gut.

CHAPTER 3

Interviews: Showing Them Why You're the One

An interview isn't just about them choosing you... it's also about you choosing them.

YOU'VE NAILED WHAT job adverts are *really* saying and crafted a CV that grabs attention. You've applied smart, and not at random. Now, you've landed an interview, which means it is just one more hurdle to overcome before all that effort can start to pay off.

An interview is not an exam. It's not about giving perfect answers or pretending to be someone you're not. Employers bring you in because they already think you might be right. Now they want to find out more about you, your experience, to see if you'll fit the role, the team, and the office vibe. Just like when the employer was reviewing your CV, they're asking themselves one main question:

Can I trust this person to show up, do the job and make my life easier?

Your job is to make that answer a confident, undeniable 'Yes!'.

In this chapter, I'll show you how to do that.

Know the Role Better Than the Job Advert

Before your interview, go back to the job advert and highlight the skills, tasks and key words mentioned. They may have also given you a 'person specification'. This sets out the skills, experience, behaviours and qualities an employer is looking for in the right candidate (normally focusing on soft skills). Employers use it alongside the job description to assess applications, shape interview questions, and fairly compare candidates against clear criteria. The job advert and person specification are basically your cheat sheets for what the employer cares about.

Ask yourself:

- What parts of my CV match their needs?
- What examples prove I can do what they're asking for?
- What transferable skills can I bring if I've never done the job before?

Don't overthink it. As already mentioned, you don't need years of experience. School projects, volunteering, helping with family responsibilities, clubs, sports or even hobbies can show teamwork, problem-solving, time management, communication and leadership.

Employers love someone who connects the dots for them. Don't make them work to figure out why you're the right fit – spell it out clearly. Show how your skills, experience and achievements line up with exactly what they're looking for in the role. Prepare examples. When you bridge that gap for them, you make their decision easy; you're not just a candidate, you're the person they need.

For example:

The job advert says: 'We're looking for someone with strong customer service skills and good organisation, who is confident using systems.'

Instead of saying: 'I've worked in retail and I'm organised.'

Say this: 'In my retail role, I handled customer queries face-to-face and online, managed daily bookings on the system and prioritised tasks during busy periods. That experience has given me the customer service, organisation and system skills you're looking for in this role.'

This way, you're doing the thinking for them, matching their needs directly to your experience and making it obvious why you're the right fit.

Research the Employer (It Shows You Care)

You don't need to stalk their LinkedIn history or read the whole of their website. Just learn the basics.

- What does the business do?
- Who do they serve?
- What's their vibe – professional, casual, creative?
- What do reviews on Indeed or Glassdoor say?
- What impressed you about them?

This helps you answer questions with confidence and shows them you're not just applying anywhere and everywhere (even if you are).

Note: The employer may also research you. So, make sure your social media accounts are clear of any unfavourable posts.

First Impressions Start Before You Even Say 'Hello'

This is huge – and not in a 'wear a suit or else' way! It's about being prepared, calm and respectful.

Here's what gets noticed:

- Arriving 5–10 minutes early (not 30).

- Dressing in a way that fits the workplace. If you're unsure, go simple, neat and clean.
- Being friendly, but not forced, to everyone you meet, especially reception staff (they often get asked by the interviewer).
- Bringing anything they asked for (ID, certificates, portfolio, notebook).

You don't need to look perfect, but you need to look like you made an effort.

The Questions You Might Be Asked (And How to Answer Them)

Every interview is unique. It depends on the role, the interviewer… even the interviewer's mood at the time of the interview. So, don't work yourself up trying to anticipate what the employer will ask you.

Pro Tip:
There are loads of interview question examples online, so ask your search engine. Or ask someone who's experienced in interviews to do some mock interviews with you.

Here are some common basic questions many employers ask, and how to answer without sounding like a robot.

'Tell me about yourself.'

They don't want your life story. They want the work version of you.

Keep it simple:

- Where you are now (school/college/job)
- What you enjoy or are good at.

'Why do you want to work here?'

Use your research. Show them you've paid attention, even if it's just:

- You like the type of work
- You're interested in the industry
- Their values or vibe match yours
- You're looking to grow and learn.

'What are your strengths?'

Pick two or three things relevant to the role and give a quick example.

Avoid: 'I'm a people person.' Use: 'I'm good at talking to people. At school, I...'

'What are your weaknesses?'

Don't say 'I'm a perfectionist'. They've likely heard it a million times.

Instead:

- Pick something real
- Explain how you're improving it.

Example: 'I get nervous speaking in groups, but I've been pushing myself to contribute more in class and it's really helping.'

'Tell me about a time you solved a problem.'

Use a simple structure:

- Situation
- What you did
- Result.

It doesn't need to be dramatic. Everyday wins count.

An example could be:

Situation: In a group project at school, people were unsure who was doing what, and work started falling behind.

What you did: I suggested splitting the tasks clearly. I wrote them down and checked in with everyone before the deadline.

Result: Everybody knew their role, the project was finished on time and we got positive feedback from the teacher.

Pro Tip:
Nerves often cause rambling because silence feels uncomfortable, but a pause shows confidence not uncertainty. Give a clear, to-the-point answer...then stop.

Assessment Centres and Psychometric Tests

These are tools employers use to understand how you think, communicate and solve problems – it is not just what's written on your CV. You might be asked to complete online quizzes, group tasks, role plays or timed exercises designed to reveal your strengths, your teamwork style and how you handle pressure.

They're not about catching you out; they're about giving employers a clearer picture of how you work in real situations. Expect a structured, sometimes busy, environment, a mix of individual and group challenges and plenty of opportunities to show who you are beyond the interview chair.

Note: When working in a group, speak up, but also give others the chance to speak as well. Employers are looking for team players. People who can confidently share their ideas, listen to others and work collaboratively to achieve the best outcome.

The bonus? These assessments give you insights too. They help you spot your strengths, understand how you prefer to work, and identify areas you can confidently develop as you grow. The more you know about how you prefer to work, how different environments affect you and what you need to perform at your best, the more power you have to make smart choices. You can spot roles that fit you, avoid ones that drain you, and walk into opportunities knowing exactly how to show your strengths.

Your Turn: Questions You Could Ask

This is where you show maturity and confidence, not by grilling them, but by showing you care about choosing the right role.

Try:

- 'What does a typical day look like?'
- 'What would success look like in this role?'
- 'What training or support will be available?'
- 'What are the next steps in the process?'

And yes, you can ask about salary if it still hasn't been revealed, though keep it light:

'Before we go further, can you confirm the salary or pay range for the role?'

Totally normal. Totally professional.

Body Language: Calm, Confident, Human

You don't need perfect posture or to stare at them like you're in a staring contest.

Aim for:

- Sitting up (not stiff)
- Smiling occasionally
- Eye contact in natural moments (including everyone in the room, as often there'll be more than one interviewer)
- Nodding to show you're listening
- Using your hands if you normally do.

Just don't overthink it. Be the most relaxed, respectful version of yourself.

Nerves Are Normal: How to Handle Them

Everyone gets nervous. Yes...everyone.

Try:

- Taking slow breaths before you go in
- Practising answers out loud with a friend
- Planning what you'll wear the night before
- Leaving earlier than you think is necessary, just in case of traffic
- Reminding yourself: 'They already liked me enough to invite me in.' That's huge.

Pro Tip:
When nerves hit, your breath is your secret weapon. Try a breathing method like cyclic sighing. Take two sharp inhales through your nose, then release a long, slow exhale through your mouth. Repeat for 10–60 seconds, depending on your needs. Your body does this automatically when you're uncontrollably crying – it's a built-in stress reset and it works surprisingly fast.

After the Interview: Don't Just Leave and Hope

A small follow-up message can make you stand out.

Something like:

'Thank you for seeing me today. I really enjoyed learning more about the role and I'm excited about the opportunity. Please let me know if you need anything else from me.'

Professional. Simple. Memorable.

Your Path to Employment

Your path to getting hired can look slightly different depending on the employer and how they choose to assess candidates. Some roles move quickly, while others involve several stages to help the employer make the right decision.

Typically, the process starts with your CV and cover letter, followed by screening or assessments. If successful, you'll usually be invited to a first interview, and it's common for there to be a second or final interview, so don't be surprised if the process takes more than one round.

Discussions about pay and terms often happen later in the process, once the employer is confident you're the right fit. The final stage is receiving, and potentially negotiating, your job offer.

The key thing to remember is that each step builds on the previous one. Reaching the later stages means you're doing well.

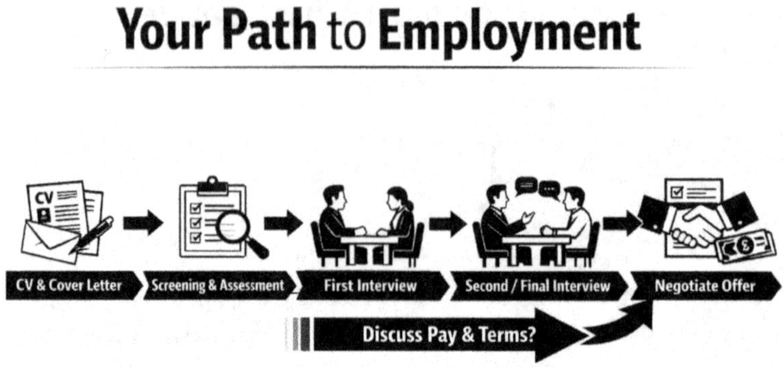

If You Don't Get the Job, Don't Panic

Rejection stings, but it's not personal. Employers juggle dozens of candidates, business pressures, deadlines and, sometimes, internal politics.

What you can do:

- Ask for feedback (even if they don't reply)
- Keep a note of what you did well and what threw you
- Keep applying. Interviewing is a skill, and skills improve with practice. Every interview makes the next one easier.

If You Do Get the Job, Nice!

But don't accept it blindly. Make sure:

- The salary meets your 'must-have' number
- The contract type fits your lifestyle
- You understand the hours and location
- You know what the role involves and what's expected of you.

Remember, a job must work for you too.

An interview isn't about being the best person in the world. It's about being the best fit for that job, on that day. You're far more capable, and far more ready, than you think.

Pro Tip:
When I started out, I carried a simple folder filled with my certificates – my own version of the old National Record of Achievement. Schools don't give those out anymore, but you can easily create your own. Every time I took mine to an interview, it impressed the interviewer...and I got the job.

With the right prep, the right mindset and the right confidence, you can walk into any interview and hold your own.

You've got this!

Up Next

Your email inbox pings/your phone rings – you've got the job! Now it's time to start work and get on the payroll. In the next chapter, I'll dive deeper into contracts. I'll also give you the key details you'll need for payroll.

Takeaways

- Interviews aren't exams, they're conversations – Employers already think you might be the right fit; now they want to see if they can trust you to show up, do the job and make their life easier.
- Know the role better than the advert – Match your skills, examples and achievements to what they've asked for, and make these connections obvious.
- Show you care by doing smart research – A bit of digging into the company helps you answer confidently and shows you're not just applying everywhere.
- First impressions matter long before you speak – Being prepared, on time and respectful set the tone for the whole interview.
- Answer simply, clearly and like a human – Use real examples, honest weaknesses and short stories that show how you work.

- Nerves are normal. Manage them, don't fight them – Techniques like cyclic sighing help you regain calmness quickly, so you can show up as your best self.

CHAPTER 4

Contracts and Getting on the Payroll

Your first shift isn't just about learning the ropes, it's about getting on the system.

YOU'VE LANDED YOUR first job. Exciting, right? Whether it's a weekend gig at the local café, a summer job, or your first full-time role, there are some things you need to consider before you start to learn the job. You'll encounter contracts (of which there are different variations), policies and procedures, and, of course, payroll.

In this chapter, I'll talk you through what happens before your first shift, from what your contract should include and how to get set up on payroll, to General Data Protection Regulation (GDPR). I'll cover the types of contract you might be offered, what to check before signing, the details your employer will ask for, and how to protect your data and your rights. By the end, you'll feel confident, prepared and ready to step into working life.

Understanding Contracts

A job starts with an employee contract. If you're not provided with one when you start, then ask.

The word 'contract' might sound intimidating, but it's simply an agreement between you and your employer. It sets out how much you'll be paid, your working hours, your holiday entitlement, benefits, responsibilities and the standards you're expected to follow. Think of it as the guidebook to your working life; the rules of the game, so everyone knows where they stand.

Don't zone out just yet...contracts aren't just boring paperwork. They protect you as much as they protect your employer. Without one, it's like playing football without any rules...and no one wants that chaos, do they?

There are different types of employee contract. It's important to know which one you're on, because each comes with its own set of expectations. Let's look at the main contract types you're likely to come across as you start your working life.

All contract types provide you with:

- Paid holidays – You'll get time off to rest (once you've reached school-leaver age). I'll go into holidays more in Chapter 8.
- Sick pay – If you're ill and can't work, you still get paid. It matters because even when you're unwell, your bills don't stop, and having sick pay means you're protected while you recover. I'll explain this in Chapter 8.
- Pension contributions – If you're in a workplace pension scheme, you'll get some money from your employer to top up your pension for when you retire. I'll go more into pensions in Chapter 9.

But there are differences...

Permanent Full-time Contract

This is the big one. If you're on a permanent full-time contract, congrats, you've got hours security! Full-time means you're probably working 35–40 hours a week and five days per week. You sometimes get more than the minimum benefits mentioned above. Such a contract is normally paid as a salary.

Permanent Part-time Contract

Not ready for the full-time grind just yet? No problem. Part-time contracts are similar to full-time ones in terms of rights and perks, but with fewer hours. Getting a job with part-time hours allows you to fit it more around your life, say if you're still studying. Maybe you'll work three days a week or a few evenings, which also gives you the security of guaranteed hours.

The big difference is everything's prorated, meaning amounts are worked out fairly based on the time worked. Again, I'll go into this in more detail in Chapter 8. This type of contract can be salaried or hourly paid.

Fixed-term Contract

This is exactly what it says – it's a contract for a set period of time. Maybe you're covering someone's maternity leave or you're working on a project that only lasts six months. Once that time is up, so is the job. You can have a full-time or part-time fixed-term contract, but the main thing to remember is that there's an end date in sight.

While less secure than a permanent job, fixed-term contracts can be a great way to get experience, especially if you're just starting out. And who knows? If you impress, you might be offered a permanent role when your contract is up.

Ad Hoc, Casual or Zero-hour Contract

Though there are several names, it's the same type of contract. An ad hoc, casual or zero-hour contract (referred to from here as an ad hoc contract/ad hoc worker) means you're not guaranteed hours. This contract is paid as hours worked. The employer calls you when they need you. If they don't need you, then there's no work that week. It is as simple as that.

These contracts are common in industries like hospitality, retail or events. If you're working in a restaurant for example, you might be called in for a busy weekend, but you might not be needed for the rest of the week. While they give you a lot of flexibility, they can also be a bit unpredictable. Some weeks you might be working loads, while other weeks...crickets. So, if you like to plan your life and budget your money, an ad hoc contract might not be ideal.

That said, casual work can be brilliant if you've got other commitments, like studying or travelling, and don't want to be tied to a regular schedule. Unlike with a fixed-hour contract, you can say no to hours offered on an ad hoc contract if they don't fit in with other commitments. However, if you say no too often, you run the risk of being bottom of the list for future hours, and you might really need the money.

Freelance or Self-employed Contract

Freelancing is like being your own boss. Instead of being employed by one business, you're hired by different clients to do specific jobs. Writers, graphic designers and photographers are often freelancers. You'll provide your client a contract for each project, but you won't be an employee of the business.

There are strict rules on what makes you an employee of a business, and if there's a deemed employee status, employee taxes are due. This comes under regulations such as 'off-payroll working' known as IR35. If freelancing or self-employment is something you're thinking about, check out the link at the end of the book (in the Links section) for more information.

One of the biggest perks of freelancing is the freedom to choose who you work for and when. But with great power comes great responsibility. You'll need to manage your own taxes, pensions and holiday pay. No one is going to pay you for time off and there's no sick pay. It's important to stay organised, on top of your finances and seek the right advice. This means completing regular self-assessment returns to HMRC (His Majesty's Revenue and Customs). If a limited company, there are several different reporting requirements and tax liabilities to consider as well. What you need to do depends on how the business is set up. There is a variety of business type:

Sole trader: You run the business as an individual. It's simple to set up and run, but you're personally responsible for any debts.

Partnership: Two or more people run a business together and share profits, costs and responsibility. Each partner is usually personally liable.

Limited company (Ltd): The business is a separate legal entity from you. It offers more protection for personal assets but comes with more rules, reporting and admin.

Limited liability partnership (LLP): Common for professional services. Partners run the business, but their personal liability is limited.

Social enterprise/community interest company (CIC): A business set up to benefit the community or a social cause, with profits mainly reinvested rather than paid to owners.

It's important to understand what you're getting into, and the costs. Get professional guidance before going ahead.

Freelancing can be fun and rewarding, but it's not always stable. You might have loads of work one month, but nothing the next. If you like structure and a steady income, freelancing might not be for you, or maybe not full-time. You need commitment and determination to make it work.

Apprenticeships

These are brilliant ways to earn while you learn. You're employed, but you also spend time training for a qualification, splitting your time between work and study. The contract will be like a full- or part-time contract, depending on the hours (there's usually a minimum number of hours you need to be employed for), but the main difference is that the job is tied to your education.

Apprenticeships are common in trades like plumbing, electrical work or hairdressing, but these days you can find them in almost any industry, including business, IT, law and payroll. The pay might be lower to start with, but you're gaining valuable skills that will help you climb the career ladder faster.

What to Look Out For in a Contract

Now that you know the different types of contract, let's focus on what you should check before signing anything. These are the key points to pay attention to:

- Pay rate – How much you'll earn per hour or per year. Make sure it meets at least the National Minimum Wage (more on this in Chapter 5).
- Hours of work – Do they match what you agreed to? Check whether there's flexibility, whether overtime is expected and what rate it'll be paid at.
- Holiday entitlement – How much time off are you entitled to? If you're under school-leaver age, you won't have

statutory holiday entitlement yet (see Chapter 8 and the Links section for more information).

- Job description – Does the contract reflect the role you applied for? Make sure the responsibilities line up with what you were told.
- Notice period – How much notice do you need to give if you decide to leave, and what happens if your employer ends the contract?

You may receive an employee handbook, which is separate from your contract. While your contract sets out the essentials (your role, pay, hours and the legal agreement between you and your employer), the handbook explains how things work day-to-day. It usually covers policies on sick leave, pay, holiday procedures, dress code, health and safety, disciplinaries, grievances and more. It's worth reading because it tells you exactly how to do things like reporting sickness or understanding what happens if workplace issues arise.

They might not be the most exciting documents, but reading your contract and the handbook properly gives you clarity and confidence as you start your new role.

Know Your Rights

Your first job is exciting, but it's important not to let that excitement distract you from understanding what you're agreeing to.

Some employers, particularly for Saturday jobs or roles for under-16s, may not issue a formal contract. If no contract is provided, make sure the agreement is still confirmed in writing. This should cover things like your hours, pay rate, holiday entitlement and how to book holiday, breaks and what happens if you're off sick. Once you turn 16 and start working more hours, you should always expect a contract to be in place.

Having a contract is strongly recommended as it clearly sets out expectations and protects both you and your employer. By law, employers must give you a written statement of your employment details (usually a contract), so don't accept excuses or delays. Read it carefully, ask questions if anything isn't clear and be sure you understand what you're signing.

Once that's sorted, the next step is providing your details so you can be set up on the payroll.

Getting Set Up On the Payroll

Once the contract is signed, the agreement is reached. The next big milestone is getting on to the payroll. This ensures your effort turns into money in your bank account. Payroll might sound dull, technical and confusing, but it's the vital system that makes sure you're paid correctly – on time, every time. Once you understand it, it's not so bad, and is worth knowing. There's never a dull day in payroll.

Here's what usually happens. Your employer will ask for some key details:

- Your full name (this needs to be your legal name as it appears on your birth certificate, including any middle names)
- Your date of birth
- Your address
- Your National Insurance number
- Your bank account info
- A P45 if you've worked before. This is your statement of earnings from your previous employer

- If you've not worked before or don't have your P45 from your previous employer yet, they'll ask you to pick a starter declaration statement:
  - Statement A: The job is your main job, but first job of the tax year starting 6th April
  - Statement B: The job is your main job, but you have had another job since the start of the tax year but haven't received your P45 from them yet
  - Statement C: This job is your second employment (you already have another job)
- Your email address
- If you have a student loan, make sure your employer knows what plan type it is.

Such information ensures you're taxed correctly and that your hard-earned pay lands in the right place. Taking care to answer correctly and fully means you won't find yourself underpaid, overtaxed or, worse, waiting for money that never arrives.

You'll also be asked for some other information your employer will want to keep on record, such as:

- Next of kin/emergency contact – Who they should call if something happens to you at work
- Clothing size – This is relevant if you're required to wear a uniform provided by your employer.

General Data Protection Regulation (GDPR)

GDPR (governed by the Information Commissioner's Office – ICO) is a set of rules that protects your personal information – things like your name, address, school details and anything else that identifies you. Before handing over any details, ask where they'll be stored, how they'll be used and who can access them.

Employers must keep your data safe and only use it for legitimate reasons, like paying you. GDPR also gives you rights – you can see what information employers hold, correct it or ask for some of it to be deleted. In short, it keeps your personal details protected and puts you in control.

Note: Employers are legally required to hold some of your details for HMRC and government records.

Your First Step to Financial Independence

Your first day will depend on the employer and type of work you'll be doing. For a Saturday job in a café, your first day might be a chat, meeting the team and a quick show around. Larger employers may have a formal induction programme, which can include online training, such as health and safety, for you to complete.

If you're brand new to work, don't panic, your employer can guide you through all the paperwork, or you can ask someone who's got experience. Remember, this isn't a one-and-done exercise. Payroll follows you throughout your working life, so getting to know how it works early on is a smart move.

Ask questions, double-check forms and keep your payslips safe.

Payroll isn't just admin – it's the foundation of your financial life. Getting it right means getting paid right. Understanding it early puts you in control of your money, your rights and your future.

Up Next

Now you're set up and ready to go, with your contract signed, payroll details sorted and your working life officially underway, let's look at how your time turns into money and the minimums you need to know to make sure you're paid fairly.

Takeaways

- Contracts aren't scary – They're your deal with the employer and protect your rights.
- Different contracts, different rules – Full-time, part-time, fixed-term, ad hoc, freelance or apprenticeships all come with unique expectations.
- Check the details – Pay, hours, holidays, job role and notice period should all be crystal clear before you sign.
- The employee handbook explains the day-to-day rules that keep the workplace running smoothly.
- Payroll matters – The information you give upfront ensures you're taxed correctly, paid on time and equipped with payslips that help you rent, borrow and build your financial future.
- GDPR protects your personal information and gives you control over how others store, use and access your data.

CHAPTER 5

Time, Money and Minimums

Your time is literally money, but how much is it worth at the very least?

TIME IS WHAT you trade when you work for an employer, but most people rush into their first job without really understanding how that time is counted, what it's worth or how it turns into actual money. That's where problems start. Missed hours, unfair pay, confusing payslips and wages that don't match what you expected.

This chapter gives you the clarity most people don't get until they've already lost out. It's about understanding the link between your time and your money. I'll start with clocking in and out, how your hours are recorded and why accurate tracking matters, before breaking down minimum wage, how it changes with age, how your pay is calculated and why knowing your hourly rate puts you in control. It's not just about the bottom line. It's about valuing your time, spotting unfair deals, reading your payslip confidently and making sure you're never short-changed.

Time, money and minimum rates are the foundations of every payslip. When you understand how your hours turn into the money you've earned, you gain the confidence to notice when something's off, speak up when it is and take ownership of your working life, your finances and, ultimately, the lifestyle you want to build.

Every job has a value attached to it. Sometimes the job is hourly paid; other times it is calculated annually. Either way, time is literally money. Hourly workers are paid for each minute worked, while salaried workers receive a fixed amount split evenly across the year regardless of exact hours. Sitting beneath all of this are the legal minimums: the National Minimum Wage (NMW) and, as you get older, the National Living Wage (NLW). These set the lowest legal amount you can be paid for your time, and employers must follow them. Starting on minimum wage is completely fine and expected – it's a launchpad – but the key is knowing where you stand, what you're owed and how your pay should grow as your skills and responsibilities increase.

Clocking In and Out: How Your Hours Are Tracked

Before you get paid, your employer needs an accurate record of the hours you've worked. This begins with clocking in and out. Depending on the job, this might be a swipe card, a fob, an app, a fingerprint scanner or signing off a weekly timesheet. Some workplaces use rotas or fixed schedules.

If you're on a salary, you may not need to clock in and out at all, but it's still important to keep your own record. The Working Time Regulations set limits on maximum hours, rest breaks and things like the 48-hour rule, so knowing your time matters even when you're not hourly paid. Make sure you take the rest breaks you're entitled to; those short pauses in your day help you recharge, stay focused and perform at your best for the rest of the day. If you've been putting in extra hours, make sure your pay isn't dipping below the minimum rate if you're on a salary.

Whichever system your employer uses, the principle is the same: it records the start and end of your working time, so you're paid correctly. That's why accuracy is essential. Forget to clock in and the system may show you never worked. Forget to clock out and it might look like you worked through the night, until someone rejects it and you have to fix the mistake.

Pro Tip:
Treat your timesheet like your payslip. It is personal, important and worth protecting. Always check your recorded hours before they're approved. A missing 15 minutes here and there adds up quickly. The more careful you are with clocking in and out, the smoother payday will be.

Clocking in and out isn't just about logging time; it's about building reliability. Being consistent shows your employer you take your role seriously and saves you from unnecessary hassle when payday arrives.

Time: Why Every Minute Matters

Your working hours can be tracked in two main ways:

Clocking In and Out

This logs your exact start and end times. Some systems track to the second; others round to the nearest few minutes.

- Check your hours regularly.
- Make sure early starts, late finishes or job-specific prep time are recorded as they count as paid work.

Rota or Scheduled Hours

Common in retail, hospitality and care. You're given a set rota and expected to work those shifts.

- If you start early or stay late, make sure it's logged.
- Never assume staying late automatically means more pay – if it isn't authorised or recorded, it may not count.

Not all time is paid. For example, in the UK, shifts of six hours or more legally include a 20-minute unpaid break unless your employer chooses to pay it. That means a 9am–5.30pm shift with a 30-minute break is only eight paid hours.

Your time is your value, so track it.

Getting on to payroll and tracking your hours accurately are the nuts and bolts of working life – the practical foundations that make sure you're seen, counted and paid. Once you've got that down, the question of how those hours turn into actual pounds in your bank account is simple. That's where pay rates and minimums step in.

Money: How Your Hours Turn into Pay

Once your hours are recorded, your pay depends on the type of contract you're on, as discussed in Chapter 4.

Hourly Paid

This is where every hour counts. If you work 15 hours, you're paid for 15 hours. If you work 37.5 hours, that's what you're paid for. Simple.

- Great for flexibility.
- Easy to match hours to pay.
- Can be fixed weekly hours or change week to week if on an ad hoc contract, making budgeting a bit trickier.

Salaried Pay

This is where you're paid a fixed amount per year, split into monthly wages. For example, if you earn £24,000 a year, that's £2,000 per month before deductions. (**Note:** This is important. I'll discuss deductions more in Chapter 7.)

- Predictable and stable.
- Sometimes includes extra benefits, like health insurance.
- You might be expected to work extra hours without extra pay.

Either way, your payslip should show how those hours, or that salary, turned into your earnings. Understanding your pay structure helps you spot mistakes, understand overtime and recognise when something doesn't look right.

Minimums: Know the Legal Floor

The National Minimum Wage (NMW) and National Living Wage (NLW) set the lowest legal hourly rates you can be paid, and they're based on your age. These rules start from the age of 16, so if you're under 16, there's currently no legal minimum an employer has to pay you. The rates usually rise each April and your employer must apply any increase from the first pay period that begins on or after the change.

I'll not detail what they are, as by the time you're reading this book they've probably changed, but if you enter 'National Minimum Wage and National Living Wage rates' into your search engine and the year that the tax year starts in (for example, 'National Minimum Wage and National Living Wage rates 2026' for tax year 2026–2027) and select the Gov.uk option, you can find out what they currently are and have been.

What matters is not the date you're paid, but the dates you worked.

For example:

If you turn 21 on 10th September and become eligible for the NLW, but your pay period runs 16th August to 15th September, your new rate won't appear until your October payslip because that's the first pay period that begins on or after your birthday.

Starting on minimum wage is nothing to be ashamed of – we all do; it's our entry point. As your skills, experience and responsibility grow, your pay should grow too. Knowing your rights helps make sure you're paid correctly.

Your Rights: Protecting Your Pay

It's not enough to be on the correct rate. You also need to be paid for the right hours, with no unlawful deductions that push your pay below minimum wage.

Underpayment can happen when:

- You're charged for your uniform or required training
- Required training time isn't paid
- You must arrive early or stay late without it being logged
- You're paid from your scheduled start not your actual start
- Breaks are deducted incorrectly
- Salary exchange schemes reduce take-home pay below minimum wage
- Apprenticeship rates are applied incorrectly.

Any situation where your effective pay drops below the legal minimum is unlawful.

Always keep your own paper trail:

- Save payslips
- Screenshot rotas and approved hours
- Note down anything unclear
- Ask questions early.

If something doesn't look right, speak up. Mistakes happen, but being silent can cost you money. More on this in Chapter 10.

Your time has value. The clearer you are about how it's tracked, how it's paid and what you're legally entitled to, the easier it is to protect your earnings and build a working life that works for you.

Up Next

Now that you've got a solid grasp on how your time turns into money, and the minimum you're legally entitled to, it's time to look at where all that information shows up – in your payslip. I'll now break down what your payslip means and why it's important.

Takeaways

- Know how your hours are tracked (clocking in and out, timesheets, rotas) and keep your own record.
- Understand the type of pay you're on, whether hourly or salaried, and how it affects the money you take home.
- Check that you're earning at least the legal minimum.
- Spot common causes of underpayment, like missing hours, unpaid training, uniform costs or unauthorised deductions.
- Use your payslip as a tool not just a formality – It's your proof and protection.
- Speak up early if something looks wrong – Mistakes happen, but staying silent can cost you.

CHAPTER 6

Payslips Decoded

Think of your payslip as the Spotify Wrapped of your wages. It's not just a bunch of numbers; it's your money story.

YOU'VE DONE THE work. You've seen the money land in your account. Now there's one more important thing – your payslip.

Whether it's handed to you on paper, emailed to you or accessed through a staff portal or payroll app, that slip of paper (or PDF) isn't just boring admin – it's your money in code. It shows how your wages were calculated, what was taken off and what you get to keep. It's like a receipt for your pay. This chapter talks you through how to read a payslip so you can spot what's right, what's missing and what every deduction means.

Let's break it down.

What's a Payslip?

A payslip is an official summary of your earnings for a specific pay period. It's a legal requirement. If you're employed, you must get one for every payday.

Payslips come in a variety of shapes and sizes, depending on the payroll software your employer uses, though they must all have certain information on them. An example payslip is shown on the next page.

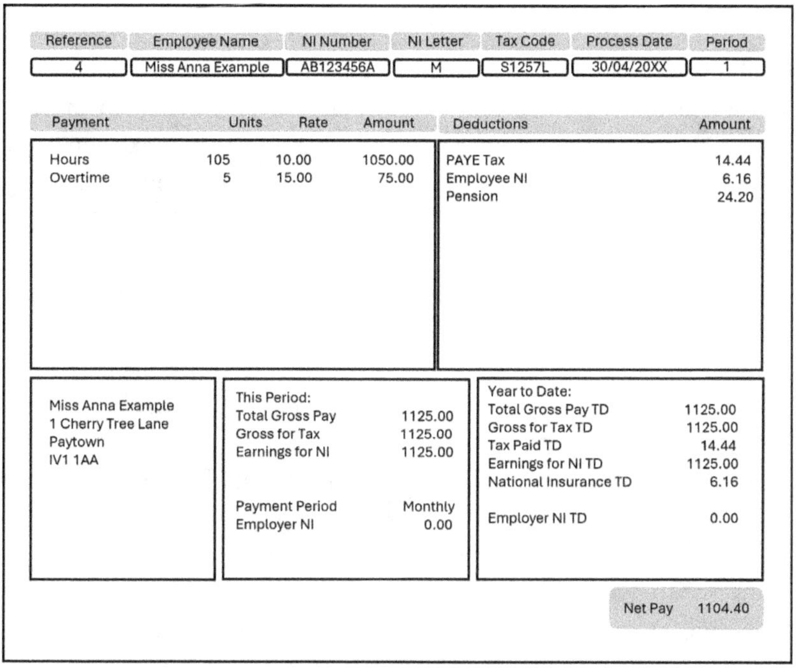

Reference	Employee Name	NI Number	NI Letter	Tax Code	Process Date	Period
4	Miss Anna Example	AB123456A	M	S1257L	30/04/20XX	1

Payment	Units	Rate	Amount
Hours	105	10.00	1050.00
Overtime	5	15.00	75.00

Deductions	Amount
PAYE Tax	14.44
Employee NI	6.16
Pension	24.20

Miss Anna Example
1 Cherry Tree Lane
Paytown
IV1 1AA

This Period:

Total Gross Pay	1125.00
Gross for Tax	1125.00
Earnings for NI	1125.00
Payment Period	Monthly
Employer NI	0.00

Year to Date:

Total Gross Pay TD	1125.00
Gross for Tax TD	1125.00
Tax Paid TD	14.44
Earnings for NI TD	1125.00
National Insurance TD	6.16
Employer NI TD	0.00

Net Pay 1104.40

Here's a quick payslip jargon buster. (Check out the Jargon Buster section at the end of the book for more.)

Term	Meaning
Gross pay	Your total pay before deductions.
Net pay	Your take-home pay after deductions.
Tax code	Tells your employer how much tax to deduct.

Term	Meaning
NI number	Your personal National Insurance number. (Think of it like your HMRC account number.)
NI letter	Tells your employer how much NI to deduct and contribute for you.
TD	To-date – totals for the current tax year (starting 6th April).
Pension contribution	Money saved for your retirement (often shown on the payslip as the pension provider's name).
Student loan	The deduction to pay back a loan you took out while learning.
Gross for tax	The proportion of your gross pay that is taxable.
Earnings for NI	The proportion of your gross pay that is subject to NI (NIable earnings).

Pro Tip:
As soon as you get it, check it! Mistakes can affect your pay or deductions. It's far easier to fix an error when it's identified early on.

The Main Parts of a Payslip (And What They Mean)

Your payslip shows:

- What you earned
- What's been deducted (like tax and National Insurance)
- What's left – your net pay (take-home pay)
- Useful details like your tax code, NI letter, payment date and employee number.

Let's break this down further and identify what you'll typically find on a UK payslip, and what to look out for.

Personal and Employer Details

These usually include:

- Your name
- Your address

    (**Note:** Even though your address is noted on your payslip, if you change your address you still need to contact HMRC yourself to advise them of the change)
- Employer's name – This might not always be the same as their trading name
- Employee number, reference or payroll ID
- NI number – You only get one of these when you turn 16. You usually get your NI number automatically in the mail a few months before your 16th birthday if your parents/guardians receive Child Benefit. If you don't get it, you can call the National Insurance helpline on 0300 200 3500. Your NI number is made up of two letters, six numbers and ends with either A, B, C or D (for example, AB123456A)

- Tax code – It's your responsibility to ensure your tax code is correct. If you're not sure, check with your payroll team first, then HMRC
- Pay date and pay period (for example, '1st–31st May') – This is not a requirement but is often seen.

Earnings (Your Income)

Here's where you see what you've earned:

- Basic pay/salary – This is your core wage, based on your hourly rate or annual salary
- Hours worked – If you're hourly paid, it should show how many hours you've worked and the rate you're being paid at (this is a legal requirement). If you're paid by the day, this will be days worked
- Overtime – Extra hours you've worked, sometimes paid at a higher rate (if applicable)
- Bonuses/commissions – Extra pay based on performance or hitting targets (if applicable)
- Other pay – Things like holiday pay, sick pay or shift allowances
- Gross pay is the total before anything is taken off. Think of it as your 'headline' earnings.

Deductions

This is where money starts coming off your gross pay, but for good reason.

Statutory (Compulsory) Deductions – more on these in the next chapter:

- Income tax – Based on how much you earn and your tax code
- NI – Based on how much you earn and your NI letter (different from your NI number)
- Student loan repayments – If you've been to university and are earning over the threshold. The deduction depends on the type of plan
- Pension contributions – Once you become eligible (more on this in Chapter 9). Automatically taken if you're enrolled in a workplace pension scheme. This can be a voluntary deduction if you're not eligible for auto-enrolment but are entitled to opt in.

Voluntary Deductions (If You've Opted In):

- Union fees – If you've joined a union
- Other deductions – Could be charity donations, cycle to work scheme, or repayments if you've had an advance or loan from your employer.

Keep an eye on what's being taken off. If it doesn't make sense, ask your manager/payroll team.

Net Pay (Take-home Pay)

This is what lands in your bank account.

Net pay = gross pay – deductions.

This is your 'real' pay – the money you can spend, save or live off.

Year-to-date (YTD) Totals

Many payslips include the current tax year's running total of:

- How much you've earned
- How much tax, NI and pension you've paid so far.

This helps you track your income and understand your position regarding tax or student loan repayments.

Employer Contributions and YTD Totals

Over and above your gross pay, your employer has amounts they need to pay for you. These are:

- Employer's NI – You've paid your NI contributions, but your employer also needs to pay NI for you
- Employer's pension – Again, you've paid your contribution towards your retirement, but your employer also needs to contribute to your pension pot. This is only if you're enrolled into the pension scheme, either through auto-enrolment or you've opted in.

As mentioned, your payslip may be given to you on paper or you might be set up for electronic payslips (often called ePayslips). With ePayslips, you'll receive login details for a secure website where your payslips, your P60 and, sometimes, other documents are stored.

At the end of each tax year (5th April), you'll receive a P60 by 31st May. This shows your total earnings and tax for the year and should be kept for your records and used for self-assessments, if you're required to complete these.

If you use ePayslips, always download and save your payslips and documents when you leave a job, as access to the system is usually closed after a period of time.

Why Payslips Matter

Payslips might not look exciting, but they're very important. They help you:

- Spot mistakes in your pay (yes, they happen!)
- Understand if you're being paid the right minimum wage
- Prove your income (for renting, loans, benefits, mortgages etc.)
- Check what tax and NI you've paid
- Track your hours and holiday pay
- Feel more in control of your money.

So, what red flags do you need to watch out for:

- Name and address errors
- Missing hours
- Incorrect tax code – Most people start on an emergency (standard) tax code, which can change each tax year. If your tax code needs to be different, HMRC will usually write to you to explain the change
- Incorrect NI letter
- Deductions you don't understand
- Pay items not added
- No payslip at all.

Know what you've earned. Know what it means.

Your payslip isn't just paperwork – it shows that you've worked, earned, contributed and are building your financial future.

Learn to read it. Question it if it doesn't look right. Never be afraid to ask what something means. The more you understand your pay, the more you can support your employer and payroll team in getting it right. If you don't understand your payslip, you don't fully understand your pay.

Up Next

Payslips tell you what you're paid, but not why the numbers look the way they do. Behind your payslip is a system of deductions, like tax and NI, quietly ticking away. Let's pull back the curtain and see how it all works.

Takeaways

- Gross vs net – Gross pay is before deductions; net pay is what hits your bank.
- Deductions matter – Tax, NI, pensions and student loans should all make sense.
- Check the details – Hours, tax code and deductions are all prone to error.
- Keep a paper trail – Payslips prove your income for renting, loans and more.
- Knowledge = control – Understanding your payslip puts you in charge of your money.

CHAPTER 7

Tax and National Insurance, and the System Behind Them

Let's crack open the mysteries of tax and National Insurance (NI), and the hidden system shaping your pay.

WELCOME TO THE not-so-glamorous but essential part of getting paid, understanding how the government takes its slice before your money hits your bank account.

Taxes might feel like money disappearing into a black hole, but there's a system behind the numbers. Here I'll give you the lowdown on tax codes, NI etc. and why what looks like 'less pay' on your payslip is about how the whole system works.

If you've ever looked at a payslip and thought, 'Where's the rest of my money gone?', this chapter is for you.

Why Do We Pay Tax and NI?

When you earn money from working, a portion of your earnings goes to the government. This isn't just to annoy you; it funds things like:

- The NHS – Free healthcare? Yes please! But it's not free and needs to be paid for
- Schools and education
- Roads, transport and local services
- Welfare benefits and pensions.

It's part of living in a society. We all chip in.

What Gets Taken from Your Pay?

Let's look at the four main deductions most people will see from their wages:

- Income tax (generally referred to as 'tax')
- NI
- Student loan repayments (if you've received a loan at university/college)
- Pension.

I'll discuss pensions in more detail in Chapter 9, but let's unpack the others here.

Income Tax: What Is It and How Is It Calculated?

Income tax is a tax on your earnings. You only pay it once you earn more than a certain amount in a tax year (6th April – 5th April). This amount is called your Personal Allowance – it's the bit you can earn tax-free.

Once your earnings go over that allowance, anything above it is taxed. The more you earn, the more tax you pay, based on different tax bands. The tax band used for your calculation is dependent on where you live (for example, Scotland, Wales or the 'Rest of the UK'). Each have their own tax bands and rates. Making sure you're in the right tax band and on the correct tax rate is crucial.

Good to Know: Your employer calculates and deducts income tax for you. You don't have to do anything to calculate it, but you do need to know if it's right.

What affects your income tax?

- Your tax code
- Your total earnings from all jobs

- Any benefits or extra income (like bonuses or company cars)
- Whether you have more than one job.

Let's go into a bit more detail on tax codes, as they have a big effect on your take-home pay.

Think of your tax code like a postcode. A postcode narrows down where a house is located. A tax code does the same for your pay – it tells your employer how much to deduct.

The numbers and letters in your tax code show how much of your income you can earn tax-free and whether anything special applies to you.

Like a postcode, your tax code can be broken down into distinct sections to determine the right tax deductions for you.

The prefix (or lack of)	There are currently three options – 'S' for Scottish tax residents; 'C' for Welsh tax residents; or nothing for the 'Rest of the UK'. This determines the tax tables your employer should use for you.
The numbers	These tell your employer how much Personal Allowance you're to receive (the amount you can be paid before tax becomes due).
The suffix	This is the letter at the end of the tax code. 'L' is the standard letter for most tax codes. Though you could have 'T' if it's a temporary tax code or 'P' when you're older and it's a tax code for your pension. 'M' or 'N' are for Marriage Allowance.

The tax code basis	If your tax code doesn't have anything after it, then it's on a cumulative basis. This means, every pay run, your tax is being calculated back to the beginning of the tax year, calculating your tax due to date then deducting the tax you've already paid – the difference being deducted in the current pay run. If a Week 1/Month 1 (or 'W1, M1', 'W1/M1', 'Week 1 or Month 1'), your tax is being calculated using only the taxable pay in the current pay run, ignoring previous pay runs.

The emergency tax code is currently 1257L (for tax year 2026–2027). Though currently frozen due to the lasting effects of Covid-19, this will change in future tax years and is the tax code that everyone – no matter where you live – starts with. It's then changed in line with your personal circumstances.

Example: Let's take a tax code of S1257L W1/M1.

The 'S' tells us that the employee is a Scottish resident, therefore the Scottish tax tables, bands and rates must be used.

↓

The '1257' tells us how much Personal Allowance the employee gets. You then add a '9' to the end, so in this case it would be '12579', meaning you'd receive £12,579 tax-free for the tax year. This Personal Allowance is broken down into a monthly, four-weekly, fortnightly or weekly Personal Allowance, dependent on your pay frequency.

↓

The 'L' tells us it's a standard tax code.

↓

The 'W1/M1' tells us that previous taxable pay and tax paid is not considered in the calculation.

National Insurance: What Is It and Why Does It Matter?

NI isn't quite the same as tax, but it still gets deducted from your pay. Unlike tax, you also have employer contributions.

NI contributions go towards your State Pension, Statutory Sick Pay (SSP), Statutory Maternity Pay (SMP) or Statutory Paternity Pay (SPP), and other benefits. To get access to the State Pension in the future, you need to build up enough qualifying years of NI contributions.

How It's Calculated

You start paying NI when you turn 16 – up to the State Pension age – and when your weekly or monthly earnings go over a certain limit. The limit for an employee's NI is known as the primary threshold (PT). The employer's NI is known as the secondary threshold (ST).

The NI deduction is then calculated as a percentage of your earnings above this limit. That percentage is set by the government and, if you're a higher earner, it drops to a lower rate on any income above the Upper Earnings Limit (UEL).

Again, your employer calculates and deducts NI automatically, but the amount changes depending on your earnings. If you work part-time, freelance or have gaps in employment, your NI record may be incomplete (which can affect your pension later in life).

HMRC has tables, which you can find on the Gov.uk website. They change each tax year, so use your search engine and type in 'NI rates and thresholds' and the tax year (for example, 'NI rates and thresholds 2026–2027' for the 2026–2027 NI rates). These tell your employer how much to take and when, and this is governed by your NI letter.

NI letters are little codes on your payslip that tell your employer how much NI you should pay, and how much your employer should pay for you. Different letters have different rules. For example, if you're under 21, over State Pension age or in a special type of job, NI might be less or nothing at all for you, but not necessarily for your employer. See below for some of the most common NI letters.

Common Letters	Who It's For	Employee NI	Employer NI
A	Most employees	Standard rate	Standard rate
M	Employees under 21	Standard rate	No NI until UEL then standard rate
C	Employees over State Pension age	No NI	Standard rate
H	Apprentices under 25	Standard rate	No NI until UEL then standard rate

Common Letters	Who It's For	Employee NI	Employer NI
X	People under 16, or not paying NI	No NI	No NI

Pro Tip:
You can check your NI record on your personal tax account (make sure you set this up) on the Gov.uk website to see how many qualifying years you've got.

Don't be surprised and miss out. Find out and benefit from forward planning.

A personal tax account (PTA) is your online HMRC portal where you can view and manage everything related to your tax in one place – things like your tax code, National Insurance record, income history and any rebates or payments you're owed. It's free to use and helps you to keep your details up to date so you're paying the right amount of tax. To set one up, go to the Gov.uk website, create a Government Gateway user ID by verifying your identity using things like your passport, driving licence, payslip or P60. (See the Links section for further guidance on set up.) Once verified, you'll be able to sign in anytime to check your tax information quickly and securely.

Pro Tip:
Keep an eye on your NI for State Pension eligibility, but don't rely on it. The government is struggling to keep it funded, the State Pension age is rising, and its future is uncertain. Plan your finances as if it won't be there. Pay into an employer/personal pension and build your own savings. If it's still around when you retire, that's a bonus.

Student Loan Repayments: Paying It Back When You Earn Enough

If you've taken out a student loan for university or college, repayments are usually taken from your wages once you earn over a set threshold, which depends on your loan type and typically changes at the start of each tax year. You can choose to make voluntary repayments. Although, consider carefully your personal and financial position and how they may change. Don't make voluntary repayments if you don't expect to fully repay your outstanding balance by the end of the loan term. Your repayments are based on how much you earn, not just how much you borrowed. See the Links section for more information.

There are different types of student loan (plan type), dependent on when and where you studied. Each student loan has its own rules for:

- When repayments start
- How much you repay
- What happens if you never pay it all off.

Repayments are:

- Automatically taken from your wages once you earn enough
- A percentage of the amount you earn over the threshold
- Stopped if your income drops below the threshold again.

Good to Know: Student loan repayments don't affect your credit score and if you don't earn enough, you don't pay.

This is not free money though, it's a debt to be repaid, so think carefully about how much you need to borrow.

The System Behind It All: PAYE

So, how does all of this happen?

The system that calculates and deducts your income tax, NI and student loan before you get paid is called PAYE (Pay As You Earn).

Here's how it works:

- You get a job
- Your employer registers you with HMRC
- Your tax code is determined, which tells them how much Personal Allowance you're entitled to. The P45 or starter declaration you provided (see Chapter 4) will determine the tax code you're set up on. This can be adjusted by HMRC, shifting with your personal tax circumstances, or uplifted if the standard Personal Allowance is changed by the government.

Every time you get paid, your employer:

- Looks at how much you've earned

- Works out the tax, NI and student loan repayments
- Sends that money directly to HMRC
- Pays the rest into your bank account, minus any other deductions.

Your employer reports all this every time you get paid through a system called Real Time Information (RTI), so HMRC always has an up-to-date picture of your earnings.

It's All About What You've Earned So Far

It's important to understand that your tax is based on your earnings to date in the tax year, not what you've earned that month. Even if HMRC has given you a 'Week 1/Month 1' tax code, which only looks at the current pay period, everything is recalculated on a cumulative basis (looking at the whole tax year) after the end of the tax year.

NI only ever looks at the current pay period if you're an employee. If you're a director, it's worked out on a cumulative basis, but with the twist that you get all your primary threshold (the point where employee contributions become due) and secondary threshold (the point where your employer's NI becomes due) first. With student loan repayments, they're always only calculated based on the current pay period.

This means:

- You might not pay tax if you're under the threshold, but that can change
- If you get a big bonus or work extra hours, you might pay more tax that month
- Your student loan repayments might start or stop, dependent on if your earnings go up or down.

Quick Recap

Deduction	What It's For	Who Gets It?	When You Pay
Income tax	Public services, education etc.	HMRC	When your total earnings go over your Personal Allowance
NI	Your State Pension, NHS and other state benefits	HMRC	When your weekly/monthly income goes over a threshold
Student loan	Repaying tuition/living cost loans	Student loan companies	When your income is above the payment threshold

Exercise:

Do you recall the exercise in Chapter 1 about calculating your 'must-have' number? I mentioned that the number to calculate would be your net pay, but your wages agreed will be gross pay. Above, I've detailed the deductions that come off your gross pay to determine your net pay. There's no simple way to accurately calculate net pay from gross pay without getting deep into the technicalities of payroll calculations. There is a helpful calculator on the HMRC website that can help you estimate what your net pay is likely to be – https://www.gov.uk/estimate-income-tax –

however, this only calculates for the current tax year. Go to www.thepayrollguide.co.uk/pay-me and download my guidance on how to use HMRC's pay calculator.

Keep Track

Getting your first job, or any job, is exciting. But getting paid is about more than just your hourly rate. Understanding why money is taken off your pay and how it's calculated means you're less likely to get caught off guard and more likely to spot problems early.

This stuff might seem complicated at first, but once you get your head around it, it's just part of working life. Don't be afraid to ask questions – it's important you understand.

Up Next

You've cracked the code on tax, NI and student loans – the stuff that comes out of your pay. Now let's flip it and look at what you're entitled to receive: holiday pay, sick pay and the key rights that protect you at work.

Takeaways

- Tax, NI and student loan deductions aren't random, they follow clear rules through PAYE, where your employer calculates/deducts them before you're paid and sends them to HMRC.
- Your tax code is crucial and it works like a postcode for your pay, telling your employer how much you can earn tax-free and how much tax to deduct. If it's wrong, your take-home pay will be wrong.
- NI builds your future entitlements – It funds benefits like the State Pension and statutory payments. Your NI record (qualifying years) matters for retirement, so check it regularly.
- Student loan repayments depend on your income and how much you borrowed – They only start when you pass a threshold and pause again if your earnings drop.

CHAPTER 8

Holiday Pay, Sick Pay and Statutory Rights

Pay doesn't stop when life happens. Let's talk holidays, sick days and the rights that support you.

WHEN YOU START your first job, it's easy to get caught up in the numbers – what you earn per hour, how much lands in your bank account each payday and whether it feels like enough. But payroll isn't just about money earned for hours worked. It also covers what you're owed when you aren't at work – things like holiday pay, sick pay and other statutory rights. These are important safety nets. Understanding them means you'll know what's fair and what isn't.

This chapter explains what you're owed so you know exactly what you're entitled to. I'll break down how holiday pay is worked out, what happens when you're too sick to work and the key legal rights you have.

You'll get clear on how your holiday entitlement is calculated – whether you're full-time, part-time or working irregular hours – what sick pay you'll receive and the statutory rights that protect you.

Holiday Pay: Getting Paid to Take a Break

Everyone needs time off. By law, workers in the UK are currently entitled to at least 5.6 weeks of paid holiday each year. You need to be at school-leaver age before you become eligible. For a full-time employee working five days a week, that's 28 days. Employers can include bank holidays in this allowance – they're not paid on top. Check your contract as it should detail your holiday entitlement, when the holiday year runs from and to, and what happens if you don't use up your holiday entitlement (in most cases you lose your holiday days, so always make sure you use them).

If you're part-time, you still get holiday pay – it's just worked out pro rata (in proportion to the days/hours you work). For example:

If you work three days a week, you'll get 3/5ths of 28 days (or three days x 5.6 weeks) = 16.8 days per year.

If you work irregular hours on an ad hoc contract, your holiday entitlement is calculated as a percentage of the hours you've worked at a rate of 12.07% (this can be more if your employer gives you more than the statutory minimum holiday entitlement). For example:

Pay Date	Hours Paid	Holiday Entitlement
30th April	114 hours	14 hours
31st May	59 hours	7 hours
30th June	92 hours	11 hours

Good to Know: Your holiday entitlement is calculated each pay run and rounded up or down to the nearest whole hour.

This builds up your entitled hours or holiday accrual. Your payout is then calculated using the average hours (or can be the hours that you would have worked for that shift) and rate (if your pay rate differs, for example for a higher overtime rate) over the last 52 weeks (where you completed some work) prior to the week you took the holiday.

There's also a method for paying holiday pay as 'rolled-up holiday pay' for ad hoc workers. This means that your holiday accrued pay is calculated for the pay period and paid straight to you. So, when you take time off you won't get any holiday pay, as your holiday pay is paid to you as it's accrued. Holiday pay ensures you don't lose income while resting. Your payslip should show it clearly, either as you take it or in each payslip if 'rolled-up holiday pay'. If it's the latter, you still need to take the time off, otherwise you'll burn out.

Sick Pay: When You Can't Work

No one plans to get sick, but it happens. That's why sick pay exists.

Sick pay is not designed as full wage replacement. It's a set amount – 80% of your average weekly earnings (last eight weeks) or the weekly SSP (Statutory Sick Pay) rate (normally increased each April), whichever is lower, and it can be paid for up to 28 weeks on a rolling 12-month basis. This is the new system for calculating SSP, as previously the first three days were unpaid and you had to earn over the Lower Earnings Limit (LEL) before you were entitled. The new calculation method came into effect from April 2026. The only constant in payroll is change, so be prepared for rules and regulations to change over time. Your employer pays SSP through payroll, just like your wages.

Some employers offer more generous sick pay schemes, above the legal minimum (called 'Company Sick Pay'), which top up SSP to your normal wage or a percentage of your normal wages. Always check your contract to see what you're entitled to.

You can self-certify for up to seven calendar days. This is required in writing to your employer, normally with an explanation of your illness. This is not a legal requirement but is helpful for your employer to see if any reasonable adjustments can be made to support you at work. If you're sick for more than seven days, you'll need a doctor's note (called a 'fit note') to keep receiving pay.

Quick Sick Pay Jargon Buster

- **SSP (Statutory Sick Pay):** The legal minimum sick pay your employer must pay if you're off work due to illness.
- **Average weekly earnings:** What you typically earn per week. This is usually worked out using your last eight weeks' pay.
- **Rolling 12-month basis:** A moving year, not a fixed January–December window. It looks back over the last 12 months at any point in time.
- **Company sick pay:** An employer's own sick pay scheme that pays more than SSP (often topping you up to full or partial pay).
- **Self-certification:** Telling your employer you're sick without a doctor's note. This is allowed for up to seven days.
- **Fit note:** A doctor's note confirming you're not fit for work (or may be fit with adjustments) if you're off sick for more than seven days.

As mentioned, payroll rules change constantly, so always check the most up-to-date guidance and your contract.

Statutory Rights: The Basics You Should Know

'Statutory' means rights that are protected by law. These apply to you no matter who your employer is and they're the foundation of fair work in the UK.

Key ones you should know:

- Minimum wage – You must be paid at least the National Minimum Wage (NMW) or National Living Wage (NLW) for your age group (covered in Chapter 5).

- Payslips – You have the right to receive a payslip showing your earnings and deductions (covered in Chapter 6).
- Holiday pay – As explained in the 'Holiday Pay: Getting Paid to Take a Break' section, with 5.6 weeks being the legal minimum.
- Rest breaks – If you work six hours or more, you're entitled to an unpaid 20-minute break (covered in Chapter 5).
- Maximum hours – There are limits on how many hours you can legally be asked to work in a week (usually 48, unless you opt out) (mentioned in Chapter 5).
- Statutory Maternity Pay (SMP), Statutory Paternity Pay (SPP) and parental leave – When an employee has a child, the law provides certain rights to time off work. This is known as Statutory Maternity Leave for mothers (person giving birth) and Statutory Paternity Leave for fathers or partners. In addition, parental leave allows either parent to take unpaid time off to care for their child. If the mother/ father meet the criteria, they'll be entitled to SMP or SPP and Shared Parental Leave.

Knowing these basics protects you. If you ever feel like your employer isn't following the rules, you're not being awkward by asking questions – you're standing up for your legal rights.

Why This Matters

When you're young and starting out it's easy to think, 'I'll just take whatever hours or pay I'm given'. Knowing your entitlements isn't about being difficult – it's about valuing yourself. Employers have legal responsibilities, and good ones genuinely want to get things right.

Workplaces have a lot of rules and regulations, and sometimes things get missed. Occasionally, there are employers who don't pay what you're due, which is why understanding your rights matters. But it works both ways. There are also employees who expect more than they're entitled to without doing the work, and they use the system unfairly. This is down to individual personality and these types of people are in the minority. Protect yourself from those who don't play fair. Don't let them shape how you see everyone else who is trying to do things right.

Holiday pay ensures you can rest. Sick pay ensures you still get some pay if you're unwell, though don't abuse it if you're hungover because you went to that 'must-go party' the night before – it's not fair on your employer or your colleagues.

Statutory rights ensure you're treated fairly. Think of these as the non-negotiables of working life. If you know them, you'll spot if something feels off. Payroll isn't just about being paid, it's about being protected.

Up Next

You've got the basics covered for now – holiday pay, sick pay and protection – but what about for the 'future you'? That's where pensions step in. It's pay you don't feel now, but one day you'll be seriously glad it's there.

Takeaways

- Holiday pay is a legal right – You're entitled to at least 5.6 weeks of holiday a year (pro rata if part-time) once you've reached school-leaver age.
- Your statutory rights cover things like NMW/NLW, breaks, payslips, parental leave, rest breaks and maximum hours – These apply to everyone, no matter the employer.
- Sick pay provides a safety net – Every employer must provide SSP, although some employers offer more. Always check your entitlement.
- Your contract matters – It explains how holiday, sick pay and other entitlements are handled. Reading it carefully lets you know what you get and helps you spot what's fair and what isn't.

- Knowing your rights isn't being awkward, it's essential – These protections exist to keep you safe, healthy and treated fairly. Asking questions means you're standing up for yourself.

CHAPTER 9

Pensions and Auto-enrolment: Paying the 'Future You'

A pension is like planting a tree. You don't get the shade today, but 'future you' will be grateful for the cover.

RETIREMENT MIGHT FEEL like a lifetime away, but your payslip is already planning for it. Pensions are money you put aside now so you don't panic later. You've worked hard to earn your wages, but one day you won't be working and you'll still need money coming in. That's where pensions step in. They're basically a long-term savings pot, built while you work, that fund you when you retire. Though it might feel a million miles away right now, trust me, you'll be glad you started early.

Here's what's happening when you see those deductions and why opting out isn't always the smart move.

What's a Pension?

A pension is a pot of money you (with a workplace pension), your employer and HMRC put aside while you're working so you've got an income when you stop. Think of it like a subscription, but instead of giving Netflix your cash you're giving it to the 'future you'.

The great difference between a pension and normal savings is that with a pension you don't carry the burden alone – your employer contributes and the government adds in extra money in the form of tax relief. That's basically free money for your retirement pot.

Auto-enrolment: Your Default Starting Point

Since 2012, workers in the UK have needed to be automatically enrolled into a workplace pension if they:

- Earn at least £10,000 a year (before tax is deducted)
- Are aged 22 up to State Pension age
- Work in the UK.

Note: The above information is based on the thresholds at the time of writing. These are subject to change.

If you meet the above age and earnings criteria, your employer must automatically enrol you in an auto-enrolment approved pension scheme. Here's how the money adds up:

- You contribute a small percentage of your wages, taken automatically through payroll
- Your employer contributes money on your behalf
- The government contributes through tax relief (and NI relief if you're in a salary exchange scheme).

Your pension pot grows faster than it ever could with your savings alone.

If you're under 22 you won't be auto-enrolled, but you can usually opt in. Starting early can make a massive difference to your future finances. If you're under 16, there's no obligation for an employer to pay into a pension for you.

Auto-enrolment is one of the rare moments in life where you genuinely get free money just for being part of the system. Turning it down is like saying 'no' to part of your pay.

Note: The government is reviewing the age at which auto-enrolment should start (along with other aspects of pensions) so the age criteria may be reduced to 18 in the future.

What About the State Pension?

Alongside workplace pensions, there's also the State Pension – money the government pays you once you reach retirement age (see Chapter 7) so long as you've built up enough qualifying years of NI contributions during your working life.

At the time of writing, you usually need at least 10 qualifying years to get some State Pension and 35 years for the full amount. The State Pension gives you a basic income but it's not designed to cover everything. It's a huge cost for the government and with current pensions already under pressure, there's no guarantee it'll still be around when you retire. That's why your workplace pension is so important – it tops up what the government provides, giving you more freedom and comfort later in life.

Can You Opt Out?

Yes, you can. But if you opt out of your workplace pension you lose your employer's contributions and the government top-up. That's like saying 'no' to free money. For most people, staying in is the smarter move.

Pro Tip:
The sooner you start your pension, the bigger your pot will be when you retire.

Why Start Young?

The earlier you start, the longer your money has to grow. Thanks to something called 'compound interest' (your money earning money on itself) even small contributions in your twenties can snowball into something much bigger by the time you retire.

What is Compound Interest?

Imagine you plant a tiny apple seed today. At first it doesn't look like much, but as time goes by the seed grows into a tree. That tree produces apples and inside each apple are more seeds. If you plant those seeds you don't just have one tree anymore – you get more trees, more apples and more seeds.

Money in a pension works the same way. The earlier you start, the sooner your money has time to 'grow branches'. Interest (or investment returns) earns you money. That new money starts earning more money on top. It's like your apples growing their own trees. Your 'future you' will be sitting in the shade of the tree you planted years before.

Here's an example:

- If you put £100 into a pension at the age of 20 and it grows at 5% a year, by the age of 21 you might have £105.
- In year two, you don't just earn interest on your £100, you earn it on the £105. That becomes £110.25.
- Each year the pot grows faster because you're earning returns on your returns.
- Time makes all the difference. So £100 invested at the age of 20 and left alone until the age of 60 could grow to over £700.

- But if you wait until the age of 40 to put in that same £100, by the age of 60 it might only grow to around £265.

Let's Bust Some Common Myths

- **'I'm too young to care about pensions.'** – The above example is exactly why it matters now. The earlier you start, the less you need to put in later.
- **'I'll never retire anyway.'** – Even if you love the idea of working forever, health, life changes or just wanting more free time might mean you stop. Having money saved gives you the choice.
- **'I can't afford it.'** – Auto-enrolment keeps your contribution relatively small. Remember, your employer and the government top it up. Opting out means walking away from money you didn't have to earn.
- **'It's too complicated.'** – Your workplace pension is managed for you. You don't need to be a financial expert to benefit.

Tips For Making the Most of Your Pension

- Start early and stay in – The employer contributions and HMRC tax relief are too good to miss.
- Check your pension statements – Make sure your money is being invested wisely. Most schemes let you see where it's going.
- Don't panic if you change jobs – Your pensions don't vanish; you retain them and can combine them later if you want.
- Think of it as a safety net – Even if retirement feels far away, life moves quickly and you'll be glad you prepared.

Motivation to Keep in Mind

Your pension might not give you instant satisfaction but it's one of the smartest financial moves you'll ever make. Every payslip contribution is a little thank-you note to the 'future you', making sure you can live life on your terms long after you've stopped working.

Up Next

You know how your gross pay is built up, what your payslip means, the system behind deductions, how statutory payments and auto-enrolment work, but what do you do if something doesn't look right? In the next chapter I'll talk about how to check your pay, spot mistakes and get things fixed so you don't lose out.

Takeaways

- A pension is pay for the 'future you' – Money you, your employer and the government chip in so that you still have an income when you stop working.
- Auto-enrolment makes it easy – If you meet the criteria you're automatically signed up, with you and your employer paying in (and you can usually join earlier if you want).
- Opting out = losing free money – You don't just lose your own contributions, you lose your employer's and the government's top-up.
- Start early for bigger rewards – Thanks to compound interest, even small contributions in your twenties can snowball into a much bigger pot by retirement.

- The State Pension isn't enough – It provides a basic income, but workplace pensions top this up so you can live more comfortably.

- You don't need to be a financial expert – Your pension is managed for you and small, regular contributions now will make the 'future you' seriously grateful.

CHAPTER 10

What If It's Wrong? Fixing Problems with Pay

When payday goes wrong, don't panic – it's fixable.

MISTAKES HAPPEN – MISSED hours, wrong tax codes, delayed payments. Annoying? Absolutely. The end of the world? Nope.

Getting paid is one of the most important parts of your job, so when something goes wrong it can feel frustrating, confusing and a bit scary. Mistakes happen more often than you'd think. Knowing what to do about them is a skill worth having.

Payroll is a process run by people and supported by technology, and neither is perfect. With so many variables, legal requirements and moving parts involved, mistakes can and do happen. The good news? They're usually easy to fix. This chapter shows you how to spot when something's off and the steps to take to sort it quickly (without burning bridges at work).

Errors are more likely if you start or leave a job mid-year, have more than one job or haven't given your employer the right information, such as a P45 or the correct starter declaration.

If your deductions seem too high, start by checking your payslip and making sure your tax code matches your situation. It's your responsibility to keep this right. If something still doesn't look correct, speak to your payroll team first, then contact HMRC if needed.

If you've overpaid tax you can claim a refund. If you've underpaid, your Personal Allowance may be reduced. HMRC will let you know about any underpayment or overpayment through a P800 letter, or the adjustment may be handled automatically through your employer.

Spotting the Problem

First, you need to realise something isn't right. Here are some common signs:

- Your pay is less than expected (missing hours, wrong rate, unpaid overtime).
- Your pay is more than expected (extra shifts you didn't do, duplicated pay).
- Deductions look odd (tax, student loan or NI not matching what you expected).
- Holiday pay or sick pay is missing.
- Your payslip doesn't match your contract (incorrect pay rate, missing additions).

I once chatted with someone who got a shock from HMRC – a tax calculation letter saying he owed over £1,000 in unpaid tax from the previous tax year. It turned out he'd had two jobs, but in his second one he was on the wrong tax code. Instead of being on BR (basic rate tax on everything), he got another tax-free allowance which he wasn't entitled to. The catch? He'd never checked his payslips and that mistake cost him big. It all got fixed and his tax code got adjusted in his main job to claim back the underpayment over the remainder of the new tax year.

Pro Tip:
Always check your payslip against your hours worked, contract and bank statement, and check that your tax code is correct. It takes five minutes but it could save you weeks of stress later.

If you find something that doesn't look right, take the following steps:

Step 1: Stay Calm and Don't Panic

It's easy to jump into worry mode, but payroll issues aren't personal, they're admin errors. Maybe someone entered the wrong number, maybe the system didn't update your new tax code or maybe your manager forgot to approve your timesheet. None of these are a reflection on you.

I was working in a payroll bureau when this angry guy stormed into reception, shouting and demanding to see whoever handled his pay. The girl who'd processed it was nervous to speak with him and, honestly, who could blame her? So I stepped in. Five minutes later he'd calmed right down. Another five and I'd explained what had happened. Turns out it was a simple misunderstanding.

Step 2: Gather Your Evidence

Before you speak to anyone make sure you've got your facts straight.

Collect:

- Your contract or offer letter (what you should be paid)
- Timesheets, rota screenshots or clocking in and out records (hours worked)
- Your payslip (what you were actually paid)
- Your bank statement (when the money landed and how much).

Having these ready makes it easier to show the issue clearly, without relying on memory.

Step 3: Speak to Your Employer Promptly

Don't wait. The sooner you raise it the easier it is to fix. Start with your line manager or payroll team. A good approach is to be polite but clear:

'Hi. I just checked my payslip and I think there's an error. I worked 30 hours last week but only 20 are showing. Could we please look into this?'

Being specific makes it easier for them to act quickly.

Step 4: Give Them a Chance to Fix It

Most employers will want to sort things out fast. After all, it's their legal responsibility to pay you correctly and they value you and your work. Sometimes it can be fixed immediately; other times you might need to wait until the next payroll run. In some cases they may issue an 'emergency payment' if the mistake is significant or it's a while until your next payday.

If you've been overpaid don't ignore it. Employers will ask for the money back. If it was their error they should agree a fair repayment plan rather than taking it all at once.

Sometimes there's not been an error and your payroll team can explain what's happening so that you can understand your pay and finances better.

Step 5: Know Your Rights

You have a legal right to be paid what you've earned. Your employer can't skip your pay, underpay you or take money off unless it's for something legit like tax or NI. Most of the time it's an error or misunderstanding. Knowing your rights helps you spot the difference between a simple mix-up and something that's not okay. If your employer doesn't fix the problem after you've raised it:

- Put it in writing (an email is fine) so you have a record
- Escalate the problem to payroll, HR or a more senior manager
- If things still don't move you can contact the Advisory, Conciliation and Arbitration Service (ACAS) for free advice. They help employees resolve workplace disputes.

Why This Matters

When you're new to work it's easy to assume 'the business must be right', but mistakes in pay are surprisingly common, especially in jobs with changing shifts, overtime or bonuses. By spotting errors and handling them calmly you not only get what you're owed, you also show you're switched on and professional.

Think of it this way: If your phone bill was wrong you'd query it. Your wages are even more important – you've earned them.

Getting paid is the most basic part of employment. Mistakes happen, but now you know how to spot them, raise them and get them fixed. That's a life skill worth keeping.

Up Next

Great! You know the steps to follow if your pay is not right, along with 'The Process' of getting paid. Now I'll move on to 'The Strategy' of getting paid. In 'The Strategy' section I'll look at how you can use what you've learnt about payroll so far, to plan ahead, earn more and take control of your financial future. First, you need to know where the opportunities are.

Takeaways

- Always check your payslip – It's your pay statement, not just a piece of paper. Check every payslip and compare it with your contract, hours and bank statement to spot issues early.
- Gather evidence before raising a concern – Your contract, timesheets, payslip and bank record are your evidence pack.
- Speak up promptly, politely and clearly – Stay calm and don't get cross. Errors are usually admin slip-ups or misunderstandings and are not personal.
- Mistakes in pay happen – Missing hours, wrong tax codes or odd deductions are common and fixable.
- Know your rights – You're legally entitled to correct pay.

PART 2:

The Strategy

'The Process' taught you how the system works.
'The Strategy' shows you how to make it work for you.

THIS IS WHERE earning becomes intentional. Where your payslip stops being a boring piece of paper and starts becoming a tool, a signal, a map and a lever. Once you understand the mechanics, the next step is learning how to play the game with purpose.

This section is about shifting from being passive to being powerful. From 'I hope this job pays me right' to 'I know what I'll earn and I've got the tools to grow faster and smarter'.

I'll teach you to spot opportunities most people walk straight past. You'll learn that pay isn't just about hours – it's about value, mindset and momentum. You'll discover that climbing the ladder isn't always in an upwards direction – sometimes it's sideways, diagonally or into something completely new. You'll learn to play the long game not just the payday game, because your future earning power is being shaped right now, whether you realise it or not.

You'll find tools for making smarter choices, building transferable skills, growing your network, budgeting with confidence and taking ownership of your long-term financial future.

This is the part that transforms you from someone who gets paid into someone who knows how to get paid well.

It all comes down to your strategy.

CHAPTER 11

Spotting Opportunities

Your payslip isn't the ceiling.
It's the floor you launch from.

JOBS AREN'T ALL created equal. Some industries, roles and skills open bigger doors (and bigger pay packets) than others, but there are opportunities available in basic, starter-level jobs.

When you start earning it's easy to see a job as just that...a job. A way to cover your bills, pay for nights out or finally stop asking your parents/guardians for money. Yes, your pay does those things, but there's more going on beneath the surface. Every payslip tells a story about your hours, your effort and your potential. Understanding payroll isn't just about making sure you get paid – it's about how to find the right opportunities.

In this chapter I'll help you see where the money really flows so you can target opportunities instead of just taking whatever comes along.

Opportunity 1: Hours and Overtime

The most obvious way to increase your income is by working more hours or picking up overtime if available. But there's a smart way to approach it.

Check your pay rate for overtime. Some jobs pay your basic hourly rate; others pay 'time and a half' or 'double time' for certain shifts (bank holidays, Sundays, nights). This is up to the employer. It's an opportunity to earn more, but minimise time spent at work.

Balance pay with energy. More hours means more money, but less time for rest, study or life. The opportunity is about choosing the right shifts and not taking every single one. There are restrictions on when and how many hours per week you can work depending on your age and The Working Time Directive (which sets the guidelines for working time).

Opportunity 2: Benefits Beyond Worked Hours

Some value doesn't come with a payment notification. Payroll often includes extras – sometimes small, sometimes huge. I've already mentioned holiday pay, sick pay and pension contributions, so here are some other examples:

- Discounts and perks – Some employers offer staff discounts, free meals or travel allowances as part of your 'total reward'. Sometimes it can be free fruit. Make sure you know what's available.
- Cycle to work scheme – Fancy swapping paying for fuel for pedal power? The cycle to work scheme lets your employer buy your bike and you pay it back bit by bit from your wages before tax. That means it costs you less, you get fitter and your commute suddenly comes with fresh air.
- Benefits such as health insurance – Think of it as a fast-track ticket to the doctor. Some employers throw in private health insurance as a perk, which means if you're ill or injured you can skip long waiting lists and get treated quicker. It's not instead of the NHS (that's still free, albeit paid by NI contributions) but it can mean extra options, speedier appointments and sometimes even dental or eye care. As this is a benefit in kind, there is a cost – you pay the tax due on the value of the benefit and your employer pays Class 1A employer's NI.

Good to Know: Any benefits you're entitled to are usually noted in your contract or the company handbook.

The opportunity here is to see beyond your hourly rate. So make sure you know what's available to you.

Opportunity 3: Learning How Payroll Works

Payroll knowledge is power. If you can read a payslip confidently, understand deductions and know your rights, you're ahead of most people. This confidence can lead to:

- Better decisions about which jobs align with your pay and lifestyle requirements
- Confidence negotiating pay rises or questioning mistakes
- Future career opportunities in payroll, finance, management or business where payroll knowledge sets you apart.

Opportunity 4: Building Your Record

Your pay history builds your financial record. Lenders and landlords may ask for evidence of your earnings. Having consistent payslips helps you:

- Rent a flat
- Get a loan or mortgage in the future
- Show proof of income when applying for other opportunities (like visas).

Every payslip is a receipt for your hard work and is worth keeping safe.

Opportunity 5: Stepping Stones

Sometimes the opportunities available aren't linked to money at all, but in where the job leads or the training and skills you collect.

A part-time job stacking shelves could lead to a supervisor role. A barista role could develop into a management position.

Your payslip today might be small, but the skills, habits and confidence you build now can multiply what you earn in the future.

Why This Matters

When you're young, jobs often feel temporary – stepping stones between study or travel. But the opportunities within them are real, and if you notice them early you can make decisions that set you up for years. Payroll isn't just about money, it's about possibilities.

Think of your payslip as more than a piece of paper. It's a map. If you know how to read it, you can find the opportunities hidden inside.

Up Next

You've spotted where the opportunities are, now let's talk about how to grab them without burning out. Work smarter not harder and you'll soon see how that translates into earning better.

Takeaways

- Overtime and shift patterns can create hidden earning potential.
- Benefits like holiday pay, sick pay, pensions and discounts are part of your true reward.
- Payroll knowledge gives you confidence and power.
- Payslips build your financial record – they are a snapshot not the whole story.
- Every job, even the small ones, can lead somewhere big.

CHAPTER 12

Working Smarter, Earning Better

More hours aren't always just about more money. Sometimes, working more hours means you're more tired.

THAT FIRST JOB feels like freedom – your name on a payslip, your money landing in your account and the thrill of spending it however you like. You're in control! But pay isn't a gift, it's an exchange. You trade your time, energy and skills for wages. The better you do the job, the stronger that trade becomes. This chapter is all about why money is *earned* not handed out, and how the right mindset can set you up for bigger paydays down the line.

Earning Not Expecting

The idea that 'money is earned' sounds obvious but it's easy to fall into the trap of expecting more money just because you want it or thinking you deserve more without putting in the work. Your wage should be a reflection of the value you bring to your employer.

This is where the difference between earning and entitlement comes in. Earning means you work for your pay. You clock in (and out), do your job well and earn your wages. Entitlement, on the other hand, is the mindset that you should get paid just for showing up and paid more just because you've been there a number of years or because you think you're owed something without backing it up with hard work.

The Link Between Effort and Pay

One of the most important things to understand when you start working is that your pay is directly tied to your effort. It's not just about turning up and going through the motions. How well you do your job matters.

Here's why putting in effort makes all the difference:

Reliability: Employers notice people who are reliable, showing up on time, every time, and doing what's expected. When you're consistent and dependable you're proving that you're earning your pay. If you're late, sloppy or unreliable it reflects poorly and you can't expect to be rewarded.

Quality of work: Doing a good job isn't about doing the bare minimum. Whether you're packing boxes in a warehouse or serving customers in a café, the better you do your job the more valuable you are to your employer. This could mean working efficiently, being polite and helpful, or going the extra mile when needed. The better you do your job the more likely you are to get recognised with pay rises or new opportunities.

Attitude: A positive attitude goes a long way. If you approach your work with enthusiasm you're more likely to enjoy it and your employer is more likely to see your potential. No one likes working with someone who's constantly complaining or doing the bare minimum just to get paid.

While a great attitude can take you far, it's just as important to avoid slipping into the mindset that the world and your employer owes you something.

Avoiding the Entitlement Mentality

As you start earning money it's important to avoid slipping into an entitlement mindset. It'll limit your growth potential. Here are a few common entitlement traps to watch out for:

Expecting more without doing more: If you want to earn more money you need to show why you're worth it. Simply being in a job for a certain amount of time doesn't automatically mean you should get a raise. Focus on how you can improve your skills, be more productive or take on more responsibility. These are the things that lead to higher pay.

Don't fall into the comparison trap: It's easy to look at what your mates are earning and feel like you should be making more. Everyone's situation is different. What matters is your own progress. If you work hard and stay committed your earnings will increase as you gain experience and skills. Sometimes, taking a lower-paid job that provides great skills development can lead to more money in the long run. It's not all about what you have now; think about the long-term goals.

Taking shortcuts: There's a temptation sometimes to cut corners and do just enough to get by. In the long run, this only hurts your chances of advancing in your job or earning more. Employers notice when people do the bare minimum and it can hold you back from promotions or pay rises.

If doing the bare minimum limits your progress, the opposite is also true. There are plenty of ways to grow your value and boost what you earn.

How to Maximise Your Earnings

If you want to increase your wages over time, here are some ways to boost your earning potential:

Show initiative: If you see something that needs doing don't wait to be told – take action. Employers love workers who are proactive and can solve problems without needing constant supervision. But don't act without prior authorisation from your employer in case it affects things you're not aware of.

Learn new skills: You are in charge of your skills development – they're your skills so take ownership. The more skills you have the more valuable you become. Whether it's learning to operate new equipment, taking on additional responsibilities or studying for qualifications, increasing your skill set can lead to higher pay. Some professions require the completion of continuing professional development (CPD). This means keeping your skills and knowledge up to date through ongoing learning.

Overcoming barriers: It's worth thinking about anything that might be holding you back from performing or progressing, such as a skill gap or something you don't fully understand. Extra training or mentoring can often unlock better performance, more responsibility and higher pay. Good employers appreciate you raising this. It helps them support your development, shows you care about your work and means they can reward you appropriately.

Ask for feedback: Don't be afraid to ask your boss how you're doing and where you can improve. Employers appreciate workers who want to grow and do better. It shows you're serious about your role and eager to progress.

Stay positive: Even when things are tough, staying positive and being a team player can set you apart. Employers notice people who keep a good attitude even when work is challenging or boring.

Respecting Your Pay: It's Earned

Your payslip is more than just a number. As mentioned, it represents the time, effort and value you bring to your job. By understanding that money is earned not entitled, you'll be better prepared to succeed in the working world.

As you move through your career, whether you're in a temporary job or building towards a long-term future, remember that the more effort you put in, the more you'll get out. Hard work, commitment and a good attitude will always pay off in the end, not just in your wages but in your personal growth and opportunities down the line.

Up Next

You've learnt how to work smarter and boost your earnings. Now let's look at the bigger picture. Progress isn't always in an upwards direction. Sometimes climbing the ladder means taking a step sideways first.

Takeaways

- Pay is an exchange not a gift – You trade time, energy and skill for money.
- Effort equals earnings – The harder (and smarter) you work the more valuable you become.
- Entitlement kills progress – Expecting more without doing more holds you back.
- Focus on growth not comparison – Your path and pay will grow with your skills.
- Be proactive not passive – Take the initiative, learn new skills and ask for feedback.
- Respect your pay – It's proof of what you've earned not what you're owed.

CHAPTER 13

Climbing the Ladder (Even If It's Sideways)

Your next career move isn't always 'up'.
Sometimes it's across or even down.

WHEN PEOPLE TALK about 'climbing the ladder' they usually picture a neat, upwards path:

trainee/apprentice → assistant → manager → boss

But in real life it's messy. Sometimes climbing the ladder means taking a step sideways, backwards or even off the ladder altogether, just to find a better one.

Moving sideways into a new role, or to a different employer, can sometimes be the smartest move you make. It can put you in a position to learn faster, earn more later and find work that fits your goals.

Rethinking Promotions

Promotions are great, they can bring recognition, confidence and, of course, more pay. But they're not the only sign of progress. Not every business will have promotions available or promote quickly, and not every promotion is worth chasing. A bigger title doesn't always mean better experience or satisfaction.

True progress comes from building skills, gaining experience and making strategic moves that expand your value. Sometimes that means saying 'yes' to a sideways role that teaches you something new, or staying put a little longer to master what you're currently working on.

What Progress Really Looks Like

Seeing your friends share their new job titles online can mess with your head. It's easy to feel behind if you're not moving up every year. But progress isn't just about promotions – it's about growth.

Real progress sounds like this:

- You're learning new skills.
- You're taking on more responsibility.
- You're becoming faster, better and more confident.
- You're being trusted with bigger problems to solve.
- You're earning more, even if your title stays the same.

Employers notice these things. They value attitude, reliability and curiosity – qualities that are harder to teach than technical or hard skills. Those traits are your real leverage for long-term pay growth.

Ladders Aren't Always Vertical

Imagine you're a team leader in retail and a job opens in customer service at a bank. It pays slightly less. Would that be a step down?

Not necessarily.

If you want to move into finance, that 'sideways' step could be the one that sets you up for higher-paying roles later. You'd learn how to work with data, understand financial systems and communicate with different types of customer. That's a stepping stone – one that doesn't look flashy now but moves you closer to where you want to go.

Here are some stepping-stone examples:

Current Role	Sideways Move	Skills Gained	Future Potential
Retail assistant	Office administrator	Admin/IT/ communication	HR, Marketing, Finance
Barista	Events assistant	Organisation/ logistics	Event management
Warehouse operative	Logistics assistant	Planning/ scheduling	Supply chain roles
Fast food crew member	Sales trainee	Customer engagement/ sales	Sales manager, Account executive

The key is to collect transferable skills – the kind that travel with you no matter where you work. That's how you turn sideways steps into upwards leaps. Be mindful that a series of short roles can raise questions about commitment, so be ready to clearly and confidently explain the reason behind each move to reassure a potential employer.

See Your Payslip as a Snapshot Not the Whole Story

Your payslip shows what you've earned for the hours worked, but it doesn't tell the full story.

It doesn't show:

- The skills you're building that can boost your future pay
- The pension pot quietly growing in the background

- The experience you're gaining that makes your next opportunity even stronger
- The connections and reputation you're building along the way.

Your payslip is the receipt for today's effort. The long game is about how that effort compounds, shaping your options, your income and your future (more on this in Chapter 14).

Think in Terms of Total Reward Not Take-home Pay

Your wage matters but it's not the whole picture. Training, pension contributions, benefits, discounts, flexibility – they're all part of your real reward package. Add them up and you'll see your job pays more than your payslip shows.

Play Offence Not Just Defence...And Invest in You

Checking your payslip for mistakes is smart defence. Real wins can come from playing offence, growing your value and increasing what you bring to the table.

- Ask for training that builds your skills.
- Volunteer for projects that stretch you.
- Go for roles that challenge you, not just ones with a slightly higher wage.

These choices lead to bigger growth than chasing one-off shifts ever could. While you're building your skills, invest in your future too:

- Build an emergency fund.
- Save for travel, education or independence.
- Contribute to your pension, even if just a little.

It might not feel urgent now, but every pound you set aside for the 'future you' buys freedom, options and a little less stress down the line.

It's Okay to Move On, Smartly

Many people get bigger pay rises by switching jobs, rather than waiting years for a promotion that may not be available.

If you're in a role that challenges you, supports your growth and offers real progression, great. If not it's okay to move on. Just do it with purpose.

Before you leave, ask yourself:

- Have I learnt everything I can here?
- Is there a next step internally?
- Will the new job teach me something this one can't?
- Does it move me closer to my long-term goals?

Don't jump ship to escape boredom or frustration. Jump because it's a step towards something better.

Why This Matters

Let's say your goal is to become a graphic designer. You're currently working in a supermarket. You could:

- Start designing posters for store promotions
- Offer to help with social media content
- Build a portfolio in your own time using packages like Canva or a Photoshop alternative
- Take a course in design (plenty are free or low-cost).

You could eventually apply for an entry-level marketing or design job even if your title was never 'designer'. That's strategy.

Career growth is rarely a straight line. Sometimes you loop, pause, pivot, sidestep or step back. That's not failure – it's how people succeed. Your greatest lessons in life will come from failure. Mine have.

Don't wait for someone to hand you a promotion. Create your own version of success, one smart step at a time, even if it's not the direction others expect. It's your journey and it's up to you how you get there.

Up Next

Sideways, upwards, diagonally...you now know careers don't follow a perfect staircase. What matters most is where those steps lead. Let's now talk about the long game, how to think beyond the payslip and build pay that grows with you.

Takeaways

- A promotion isn't always upwards. Sideways moves can be just as powerful.
- Real growth is about skills not job titles.
- Stepping-stone jobs can lead to bigger opportunities later.
- Your payslip only shows today's reward not your potential.
- Play offence not just defence. Spot mistakes, yes, but equally spend energy building your value.
- It's okay to move on – just do it with intention.

CHAPTER 14

The Long Game: Thinking Beyond the Payslip

Payday is nice, but wealth is built beyond your payslip.

WHEN YOU'RE STARTING out in work, your focus is usually on the number at the bottom of your payslip – 'What did I earn this month?' This makes sense as your first paydays are exciting and real. But if you stop there, you miss the bigger picture.

As I've talked about before, your payslip is only the starting point. The real game is longer. It's about building income, security and opportunities that stretch far beyond what's paid today.

From investments to side hustles, the real money game isn't just wages – it's what you do with them. This chapter helps you to start thinking bigger than your monthly pay so you're building something that lasts.

I'll show you ways you can start building your unique pay strategy.

Build Skills That Pay Later

Want to get paid more in the future? Focus less on job titles and more on skills that earn – skills that are in high demand, hard to automate or help businesses make money.

Here are a few to look out for:

- **Digital skills:** Excel, Canva, Google Workspace, coding basics, data entry, social media tools
- **Communication skills:** Writing professional emails, phone confidence, public speaking, negotiation
- **Organisational skills:** Time management, project planning, diary and calendar control
- **Problem-solving:** Handling complaints, spotting mistakes, finding solutions, data analysis
- **Sales and marketing:** Understanding client needs, creating content, upselling

- **Leadership skills:** Emotional intelligence, dispute resolution, decision-making, teamwork, adaptability, accountability.

If your current job isn't teaching you these, look for ways to add them:

- Ask to help on new tasks.
- Watch how more experienced colleagues do things.
- Learn outside of work – YouTube, LinkedIn Learning, free or paid online/offline courses.

Pro Tip:
The more skills you collect the more valuable you become. Value is what employers reward with higher pay.

Jobs are often stepping stones. Even if your role feels 'just part-time' you're picking up skills:

- Customer service, teamwork, reliability
- Time management and problem-solving
- Handling money, systems and responsibility.

Each skill adds to your future pay power. Thinking beyond the payslip means asking: 'What am I learning here that could earn me more later?'.

The Skills Collector Roadmap

Imagine your career like a video game. Every year is a new level and your pay is tied to how many skills you've collected along the way. The first 10 years of work aren't just about earning money – they're about gathering the tools, habits and experiences that unlock better jobs, bigger pay and more freedom.

Instead of drifting from job to job, play the long game. Treat each role, project and challenge as a chance to 'collect' a skill that gets you closer to your dream job. Reliability, teamwork, leadership, negotiation – they're the coins, power-ups and secret weapons of your career journey.

By the time you've worked through levels 1–10 you won't just have years of experience, you'll have a well-stocked toolkit that makes you more valuable to employers and more confident in yourself.

The Skills Collector Roadmap is your guide to navigating those first 10 years of working life with purpose. The collecting doesn't stop at Level 10. These years simply build the habit, giving you a launchpad for the next stage of your career and pay journey.

The Skills Collector Roadmap (Years 1–10)

Level 1–2 (ages 16 and 17) → Foundations
Goal: Learn how work works.

Collect:

- Reliability – Showing up on time, consistency, professionalism
- Communication basics – Emails, customer interaction, listening
- Money awareness – Understanding payslips, tax, savings.

Pro Tip:
Try summer jobs, part-time roles, volunteering or short contracts and treat them like a lab for life skills.

Level 3–4 (ages 18 and 19) → *Exploration*
Goal: Test different roles and environments.

Collect:

- Adaptability – Switching between industries or job types
- Teamwork – Collaborating with different personalities
- Time management – Balancing study, work and personal life.

Pro Tip:
Think of your jobs, whether in retail, hospitality or an apprenticeship, as chances to expand your toolkit.

Level 5–6 (ages 20 and 21) → *Specialisation and Stretch*
Goal: Start identifying what excites you.

Collect:

- Technical/industry skills – Software, tools or processes unique to your field
- Problem-solving – Handling challenges without relying on others
- Presentation and persuasion – Pitching ideas, influencing peers.

Pro Tip:
Volunteer for projects outside your comfort zone. For example, public speaking, event organisation or data analysis.

Level 7–8 (ages 22 and 23) → Emerging Leaders
Goal: Show you can guide and take ownership.

Collect:

- Leadership basics – Mentoring juniors, leading small projects
- Networking – Building genuine professional relationships
- Decision-making – Choosing priorities under pressure.

Pro Tip:
Don't wait for a promotion to lead. Look for opportunities to take the initiative.

Level 9–10 (ages 24 and 25) → Launchpad
Goal: Build your bridge to the dream role.

Collect:

- Strategic thinking – Seeing the bigger picture
- Negotiation – Pay rises, contracts, influencing outcomes
- Career identity – Knowing your strengths, values and unique mix of skills.

Pro Tip:
Regularly review your Skills Collector Roadmap. Which skills are missing for your dream job? Go get them.

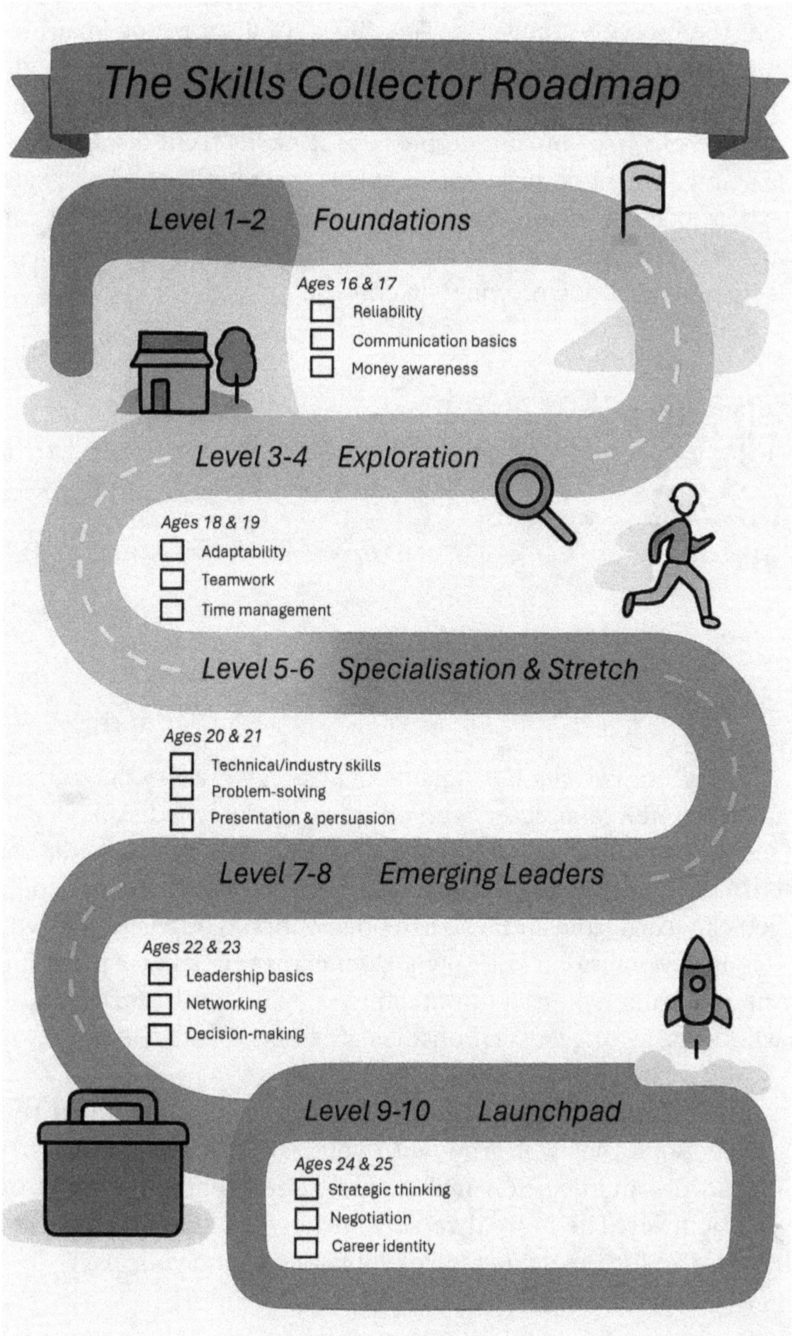
The Skills Collector Roadmap
Level 1–2 Foundations
Ages 16 & 17
Reliability
Communication basics
Money awareness
Level 3-4 Exploration
Ages 18 & 19
Adaptability
Teamwork
Time management
Level 5-6 Specialisation & Stretch
Ages 20 & 21
Technical/industry skills
Problem-solving
Presentation & persuasion
Level 7-8 Emerging Leaders
Ages 22 & 23
Leadership basics
Networking
Decision-making
Level 9-10 Launchpad
Ages 24 & 25
Strategic thinking
Negotiation
Career identity

On the previous page is The Skills Collector Roadmap for someone who goes straight into employment. Your path might include college or university. While studying can limit the hours or type of work you can do because it needs to fit around your learning, the same principles apply – you're still building skills, experience and value that support your future career. You can adapt the roadmap to your career path and circumstances. Speed it up or slow it down...you're in control.

Download:
You can download your own Skills Collector Roadmap from www.thepayrollguide.co.uk/pay-me.

Become a Connection Builder

Think of networking like a game of strategy – every person you meet is a new 'character' who can give you knowledge, advice or access to hidden opportunities. LinkedIn (the social media for business) is a great place to connect virtually with lots of people you can learn from and who can open doors to opportunities you might never find on your own. Connecting virtually is great but the real value comes from meeting people face-to-face – that's where the strongest relationships are built.

Your mission isn't to collect business cards – it's to build real connections that will grow with you. Peers, mentors, industry crossovers and decision-makers are all different 'power-ups' on your journey. The more diverse your network the stronger your launchpad for the next stage of your career (and your pay).

The Connection Builder Framework

Your career isn't just about what you know (skills) but also who you know (connections). Every person you meet can open doors to knowledge, advice and opportunities you don't yet know exist.

Core Principles of a Connection Builder

- Reach beyond your bubble – Don't just connect with people in your current job or friend group. Explore other industries, different roles and varied career stages.
- Be curious not transactional – Approach people with genuine interest and not with 'what can I get?'. Ask questions, listen and learn.
- Give before you ask – Share resources, offer help or show appreciation. Connection is a two-way street.
- Build consistency not just contacts – A connection isn't made when you click 'send connection request'; it's built when you stay in touch and cultivate the relationship with purpose.

The Connection Builder Quadrant

Think of this as four groups of people you know, each with different outlooks and perspectives that you cultivate and grow gradually as your life and experiences evolve.

Quadrant 1 Peers (same stage) – Other young people starting their careers. They'll grow with you.	**Quadrant 2** Guides (ahead of you) – Mentors, managers or experienced professionals who've been where you're going.
Quadrant 3 Crossovers (different industries) – People in totally different sectors. They'll give you fresh perspectives and unexpected opportunities.	**Quadrant 4** Gatekeepers (decision-makers) – Business owners, recruiters and leaders. The ones who can open doors when the time is right.

Download:
You can download your own Connection Builder Quadrant worksheet template from www.thepayrollguide.co.uk/pay-me

Using your downloaded copy, list the people you know in each quadrant. Identify who you're already connected with, who you could strengthen relationships with and who you'd like to meet, then go introduce yourself.

The Connection Builder Quadrant Worksheet

Write names, roles or industries in each quadrant.
Use it to track and grow your network.

<table>
<tr>
<td>Quadrant 1
Peers (same stage) – Other young people starting their careers. They'll grow with you.</td>
<td>Quadrant 2
Guides (ahead of you) – Mentors, managers or experienced professionals who've been where you're going.</td>
</tr>
<tr>
<td>Quadrant 3
Crossovers (different industries) – People in totally different sectors. They'll give you fresh perspectives and unexpected opportunities.</td>
<td>Quadrant 4
Gatekeepers (decision-makers) – Business owners, recruiters and leaders. The ones who can open doors when the time is right.</td>
</tr>
</table>

When connecting with new people The Connection Builder Quadrant works best when you focus on them first, not you. Anchor conversations around these key areas:

Context: What's going on for them right now?
Their role, studies, business, projects or current challenges.

Interests: What do they enjoy or care about?
This could be work-related or personal. What energises them?

Value: Where might you help or learn?
Share insights, resources and support, where relevant.

Experience: What have they learnt so far?
Ask about lessons, progress or what's surprised them. What would they do differently knowing what they know now?

Direction: Where are they heading next?
Goals, ambitions or what success looks like for them.

Pro Tip:
Listen more than you speak. Ask thoughtful questions and aim to build trust – not to sell or impress. Real connections grow from curiosity and relevance.

Action Steps for Connection Builders

- Attend one industry or community event per quarter (even online).
- Reach out to one new person a month with a thoughtful question.
- Reconnect with someone you already know, once a month.
- Keep a 'Connection Log' – note the date, who you spoke to, what you learnt and how you can follow up.

A 'Connection Builder' will have a diverse network of peers, guides, crossovers and gatekeepers, turning relationships into a source of knowledge, career growth and opportunity.

Why This Matters

You'll see that every payslip is a brick in the bigger structure of your working life. The habits and decisions you make alongside it – saving, learning, building experience, collecting skills and building connections – determine how much you'll earn, keep and enjoy tomorrow.

Thinking beyond the payslip is about switching from 'What did I get?' to 'Where is this taking me?'.

The long game isn't about getting paid. It's about becoming someone who always gets paid more because your skills, habits and value keep growing.

Up Next

Building your skills and network set you up for the future. But there's another part of the puzzle – managing the pay you already have. That's where budgeting basics come in.

Takeaways

- Your payslip is only the beginning – Focusing solely on what you earned this month keeps you small. Thinking long-term builds real financial power.
- Skills not job titles drive your future pay – The more useful, high-value skills you collect early on, the more doors (and salaries) open later.
- The first 10 years of your career should focus on collecting skills – Each job, challenge and project adds tools to your toolkit that enhance your value over time.
- Who you know matters as much as what you know – Building genuine relationships with peers, mentors, cross-industry contacts and decision-makers creates opportunities you can't access alone.

CHAPTER 15

Budgeting Basics: Making Your Pay Last

Your wages should work for you and not disappear the day after payday.

YOU'VE GOT YOUR payslip. The money is in your account. And for a moment, life feels great. But then the days roll by, your balance starts shrinking and by the end of the month you're wondering where it all went.

This is where budgeting comes in. Not just as a boring spreadsheet exercise but as a way of making your hard-earned money work for you. Getting paid is one thing. Making it last is a skill.

That's why this chapter lays out simple, realistic ways to stretch your pay so you can cover bills, enjoy life and still have something left for the future.

Why Budgeting Matters

Money can feel like it slips through your fingers. A few nights out, some online orders and that 'emergency' takeaway, and suddenly payday feels very far away. Beans on toast, anyone?

Budgeting isn't about denying yourself fun – it's about choosing where your money goes instead of wondering where it went.

Think of it this way: Your payslip shows what you've worked hard to earn. A budget is how you make sure that effort counts.

The Live, Enjoy, Grow (LEG) Percentage Rule

One budgeting strategy is to use a percentage rule. You assign a percentage of your income so the total comes back to 100% (the amount of your net pay).

It's easy to remember:

- % to Live – Rent, bills, travel, food, essentials
- % to Enjoy – Nights out, clothes, gadgets, streaming, hobbies
- % to Grow – Emergency fund, savings, debt repayment, pension.

For example:

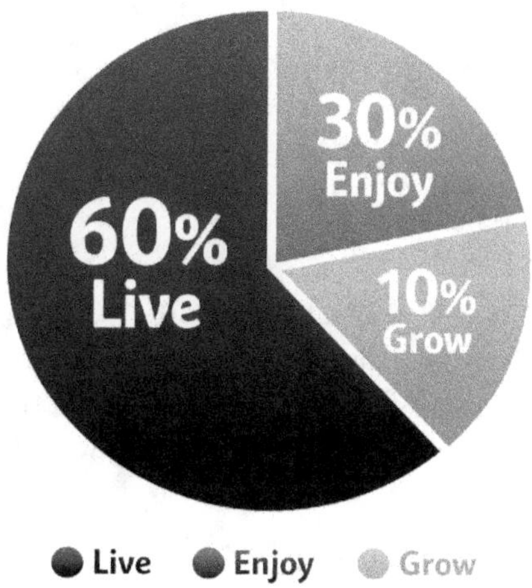

It's a great starting point. Even though the percentages will differ – and they should depending on your age and stage of life – the key message is: Choose how you split your money. Don't let it happen by accident.

You can always adjust the percentages as you earn more or your priorities change.

Live for today. Enjoy the moment. Grow for tomorrow. The LEG Percentage Rule gives you a leg up in life.

Pro Tip:
Once you've decided your percentages, move the amount for 'Grow' into a separate bank account as soon as you receive your pay. I'll explain why in a moment.

Budgeting Basics

Here are some steps to help you.

Step 1: Know Your Income

It sounds obvious but many people don't track their exact take-home pay after tax and deductions. Look at your payslip. What hits your bank account each month? That's the figure to base your budget on – not the headline gross pay.

Step 2: Track Where It Goes

I recommend for three months you keep track of every pound you spend. Use banking apps, notes on your phone or even old-school pen and paper. If this sounds too much, even tracking for one month will give you valuable insights so start there. You'll quickly see patterns:

- 'Wow, I spend more on food delivery than I thought.'
- 'Those "small" subscriptions are stacking up.'
- 'I could cut travel costs if I planned better.'

Awareness is the first step to control.

Step 3: Prioritise the Essentials

Your essentials – rent, bills, food and travel – take priority. Protect these at all costs. Falling behind on essentials creates stress, can cost more and can damage your credit score. Once they're covered you can make clearer choices with what's left.

The first part of the LEG Percentage to work out is your 'Live %' – the essentials. Everything else comes from whatever's left of your pay once those basics are covered. If it's not balanced, your good intentions won't stick for long, so next decide what percentage you want to put towards your 'Enjoy %'. But keep it realistic so you still have enough for your 'Grow %'.

Step 4: Pay Yourself First

As mentioned in the last Pro Tip, here's a trick that works. The moment you get paid move the money that you've allocated to your 'Grow %' into a separate bank account before you spend anything. Make it automatic – set up a standing order. Then you don't think about it, it just happens. Even if it's just £20, treating savings like a bill means you'll build a cushion over time. It's out of sight, out of mind and you're less likely to dip into it. Think of it as 'future freedom money'. You're buying peace of mind. The amount moved should never leave you short for what you need for your 'Live %' so you may need to start with a low 'Grow %' and then increase later.

Step 5: Leave Room for Fun

Budgeting isn't punishment. As alluded to above, if you cut out all fun spending you'll rebel against your own budget. The trick is to give yourself an allowance for the things you enjoy, guilt-free. When you hit that limit you stop. That way you enjoy today without sacrificing tomorrow.

Here are some common pitfalls to avoid:

- Living on overdraft or credit cards – It feels like extra income but it's really future debt.
- Not checking subscriptions – That 'free trial' you forgot about is eating into your budget.
- Spending as a reward for working – It's tempting to treat yourself every payday. Do it but plan it. Do not blow it.

Why This Matters

Budgeting isn't about being tight. It's about freedom. When you know where your money is going you stop feeling controlled by it. You don't panic when your balance dips. You don't dread unexpected bills. You can start saying 'yes' to things you want (holidays, cars, moving out) because you've planned for them.

Your payslip shows what you earn. Your budget shows what you keep. This difference is where financial security starts.

Remember, every payslip is the result of your effort. Budgeting is how you make sure that effort pays off. Not just today but in the future.

Up Next

Once you've mastered making today's pay last it's time to think bigger. How can you make your money work even harder for tomorrow? That's where pensions and pay growth come in.

Takeaways

- Budgeting gives you control not restrictions.
- Try the LEG Percentage Rule – Live, Enjoy, Grow.
- Track your spending for three months. It might surprise you.
- Pay yourself by saving before spending.
- Budgeting well means your money lasts longer and works harder for you.

CHAPTER 16

Future-proofing: Pensions and Pay Growth

The 'future you' is silently begging you not to ignore this chapter.

IT'S TEMPTING TO focus only on the here and now – your current wage, your next payday and what you can afford this month. Thinking about pensions and long-term growth can feel like worrying about retirement before you've even finished your probation period.

Planning ahead might sound dull but the earlier you start the easier it gets. This chapter shows how pensions, skill growth and smart choices now mean a bigger safety net (and bigger payslip) later.

The habits you set in your late teens and early twenties shape not just your next payslip but the opportunities, choices and freedom you'll have decades from now. Better money habits open more choices and give you the chance to retire earlier, on your terms. Future-proofing is about making your money work harder for you today and for the 'future you'.

Your Pension: A Quiet Benefit with Big Impact

In Chapter 9 I talked about pensions, focusing on 'The Process'. Here in 'The Strategy' section I'll look at how you can use this powerful part of your reward package to your advantage.

Look back on Chapter 9 to refresh yourself on pensions before you go further.

Your pension is a benefit that can quietly become one of the most valuable parts of your pay. Knowing how it works means you can make smarter decisions – like when to stick with the default settings, when to increase your own contributions and how to unlock extra 'hidden' pay through employer top-ups and tax relief. Your pension is a tool you can actively use to build financial freedom. It is not something that just happens in the background.

Why Start Early?

Because of compound growth – the effect where money grows on itself year after year.

Contributions made in your twenties have decades to multiply, meaning even small amounts can turn into big sums.

Remember my tree analogy from Chapter 9? Plant your pension early and it has more time to grow strong and tall. 'Future you' will thank you for the shade.

Here are some useful strategies to think about:

- If you can afford to pay more employee contributions then do so. This can be done through an Additional Voluntary Contribution (AVC).
- Instead of asking for a pay rise, it can be worth asking for higher employer pension contributions, if you don't need the extra cash right now. Increasing pension contributions can cost your employer less than raising your salary, because pay rises trigger extra employer costs like National Insurance as well as higher employer pension contributions. They could save money, you grow your pension pot sooner and compound growth can get to work.
- Rather than receiving a bonus in your pay see if your employer can divert it into your pension. As above, it could be more tax-efficient for both of you.

Pay Growth: More Than Just a Pay Rise

When you think about earning more, the first thought is usually a pay rise – getting more for what you're already doing. Some employers have annual pay rises often based on inflation (when prices rise over time meaning your money doesn't buy as much as it used to). Or pay rises are based on performance and/or experience gained. Sometimes a trade union gets involved. Trade unions are organisations that represent workers and protect their interests at work. They can negotiate pay on behalf of employees, helping secure fair wages, better terms and stronger bargaining power than individuals could do alone.

A pay rise is just one part of it. Pay growth is about increasing your income over time by making smart choices.

Ways to grow your pay:

- **Progression in your role:** Promotions, responsibility, management opportunities.
- **Skill-building:** Training, certifications and transferable skills (like IT, customer service or leadership). Remember, employers pay more for skills they value.
- **Changing jobs:** Sometimes the fastest way to grow your pay is to move to a new employer who values your skills more (research heavily to ensure you're making a smart move).
- **Second income:** Another job, freelance work, a side business or creative projects can grow your earnings outside your main job. But beware, these come with their own tax complexities so do your homework before making the leap. Check your contract too as some employers put in a clause about second employments.
- **Increased employer pension contribution:** If you receive extra pay as wages it's subjected to tax and NI at the time, whereas receiving it as increased employer pension contributions gives you the full amount to invest into

your pension. This builds your pension faster and bigger. **Note:** When you draw your pension (term for when your pension is paid out to you) it will be taxable and NIable (although you don't pay NI contributions after you reach State Pension age).

Strategy vs Short-term Wins

It's easy to think of pay growth as 'more shifts = more money'. That works in the short-term but the long game is about building your skills and career so you don't always have to trade more hours for more pay.

Linking the Two

As your pay grows, so does your freedom to fund your future. Higher earnings mean larger pension contributions, more room for savings and greater choices down the line. But remember, bigger pay also comes with bigger tax and NI deductions, and your take-home pay doesn't always rise in a straight line.

If your wage feels modest, the key is to start to:

- Put a little into your pension
- Build habits of saving and tracking pay growth
- Recognise opportunities to increase your value at work.

The combination of today's smart habits and tomorrow's bigger earnings is what truly future-proofs your finances.

Why This Matters

The amount on your payslip might feel small at present. But your future payslips and the lifestyle they support are shaped by the decisions you make today. Pensions aren't about being old – they're about giving the 'future you' options. Pay growth isn't just about money – it's about freedom, choice and progress.

Future-proofing means you're not just working for today's payslip. You're building tomorrow's security.

Up Next

You've learnt how to future-proof your money and set yourself up for long-term growth. Now it's time to bring everything together. You know the process, the strategy and the power moves, so let's end strong. In the final chapter I'll flip the switch from planning to action. Let's go get you paid!

Takeaways

- Your pension is one of the most powerful parts of your pay package. Understanding it means you can turn 'hidden' benefits into real long-term growth.
- Starting pension-saving at a young age means small contributions grow massively over time.
- Using smart pension strategies (like increasing contributions or redirecting bonuses) lets compound growth work in your favour – helping 'future you' gain serious financial freedom.
- Pay growth comes from skills, progression and sometimes moving on.
- Linking pensions with pay growth sets you up for long-term freedom.

CHAPTER 17

Now, Go Get Yourself Paid!

'Your pay isn't the end of the story, it's the starting point for your future.'

GETTING PAID SOUNDS simple. You work, they pay. But as you've seen, the process has more moving parts than most people realise. Once you understand how it works you'll shift from being a passenger to being firmly in the driver's seat.

In this book I've lifted the curtain on payroll and the pay process, showing you that money doesn't just magically land in your bank account. From spotting the signals in job ads to decoding payslips, from minimum wage to pensions, every stage of the process links back to one central point – you.

Let's recap.

The Process

CVs: When shaping your CV don't underestimate the value of all your experience. Part-time work, side hustles, volunteering – it all counts. Focus on what you've done and the skills you've gained rather than being swayed by fancy job titles. Clarity and honesty always beat fluff.

Job adverts: These can be full of shiny titles and fluffy phrases, so don't be dazzled. When you see words like 'competitive pay' read them as 'low clarity'. Dig into the details, check the small print and compare what's on offer with what you need. Treat every role – full-time, part-time or a side hustle – as something worth evaluating properly.

Interviews: Stay grounded and don't get thrown by big claims or vague promises about pay or progression. Ask questions that cut through the noise and show you're genuinely interested in the role and your personal growth. Questions like, 'What does success look like in this role?'. Show how your full range of experience, paid or unpaid, makes you the right fit.

Contracts: Your contract is your deal. It spells out your pay, hours, rights and responsibilities. Different types of contract (full-time, part-time, ad hoc, freelance, apprenticeship) carry different rules. Know what you're signing up to.

Time, money, minimums: Your time is literally what turns into your money, so the details that control how time is recorded and paid (your bank info, NI number, tax code) really matter. If you clock in and out or log hours, precision is everything. Every minute you work has a value and minimum pay laws protect that value. If the record isn't accurate you risk being paid less than the minimum you've earned.

Payslips: Don't ignore them. Gross vs net pay, deductions, pensions, student loans – every line matters. Payslips aren't just proof of pay; they're leverage for housing, credit and independence.

The system: PAYE is the system that works out what comes out of your pay before it hits your bank account. Tax and NI might feel mysterious or a bit annoying but they're part of a bigger system that keeps things running, from public services to your future benefits.

Statutory protections: Essential protections that ensure you're paid fairly not just when you're working but when you're resting, unwell or relying on basic legal rights. Holiday pay, sick pay and statutory rights are there to support you whether you're full-time, part-time or ad hoc. By understanding these foundations you can spot when something isn't right and protect yourself with confidence from day one.

Pensions: Not just for later life, your pension is a payslip for the 'future you'. Employer contributions, government top-ups and compound growth turn small deductions on your payslip into long-term security for your future. By starting early and staying enrolled you build a financial safety net that grows quietly in the background while you focus on life right now.

When things go wrong: Mistakes happen. Collect evidence, stay calm and raise issues quickly. Pay is calculated by people and technology – and both can get it wrong. There are many variables so check your payslip and act on any questions you have or errors you find.

Knowledge = confidence. Once you understand how the process works you're less likely to be tripped up by jargon, underpayment or silence. You're no longer waiting for payday to happen. You're in control of it.

But control is just the beginning. What also matters is what you do next. Pay is not just about the now. It's about growth and future freedom. This is where we step into strategy.

The Strategy

The right opportunities: A payslip isn't just proof of earnings it's a launchpad for spotting real opportunities. From choosing the right hours and understanding benefits to building payroll confidence and using early jobs as stepping stones. Every payslip reveals possibilities for earning more, growing skills and shaping your future. When you learn to read your payslip like a map you start spotting doors you didn't know were open.

Work smarter: Shifting the focus from simply working more hours to working with purpose shows that real earning power comes from effort, attitude and the value you bring. Reliability, skill-building and a positive mindset can boost your pay and open future opportunities. By understanding that every wage is earned you can take control of your growth, maximise your earnings and build a stronger future.

Climb the ladder: Reframing career growth shows that progress isn't always a straight climb upwards. Sometimes the smartest moves are sideways steps that build new skills, open fresh opportunities and set you up for higher pay in the long run. Focus on total growth and not just job titles or net pay, by collecting transferable skills, seeking challenges and making intentional moves. With the right strategy every role becomes a stepping stone towards a future you choose and not one you fall into.

Long game: Shift your focus from short-term earnings to long-term value. Show that real financial growth comes from the skills you build, the choices you make and the connections you form – not just the number on your payslip. Use my practical frameworks for collecting skills and building connections that build over time, shaping your future earning power. By thinking beyond payday and playing the long game you set yourself up to earn more, grow faster and create opportunities that last.

Budgeting: This turns your hard-earned wages into something that lasts, helping you cover essentials, enjoy life and still save for your future. Simple, realistic tools like the LEG Percentage Rule help you take control of where your money goes instead of watching it disappear after payday. By mastering this skill early you build freedom, confidence and a financial cushion that grows with every payslip.

Future-proofing: Choices you make now, especially around pensions, skills and pay growth, shape your financial freedom decades from today. Starting early, even with small amounts or simple habits, can massively multiply your future income through compound growth and smart career decisions. By future-proofing your pay you're not just earning for today, you're building long-term security, options and confidence for the 'future you'.

You now have the full picture. 'The Process' has shown you how pay works and 'The Strategy' has shown you how to make it work for you. But understanding 'The Process' and 'The Strategy' only becomes powerful when you put them into practice. Before the knowledge fades and real life takes over, here are your first steps to turn everything you've learnt into everyday action and real progress.

First Steps

If you want to turn insight into action and bring about real change, these steps will get you moving:

- **Audit your pay:** Sit down with your payslip. Can you explain every line? If not, find out.
- **Track your growth:** Record skills and hours. Each job or role should leave you stronger than before.
- **Seek opportunities:** Not just jobs. Ask, 'Does this role grow me or just pay me?'. Choose progress over stagnation.
- **Budget with purpose:** Plan your money before it arrives. Divide between Live, Enjoy and Grow.
- **Build connections:** Strong connections lead to stronger opportunities. Keep learning from others. Ask questions and stay visible.
- **Think about the long game:** Plan for pay rises, sideways moves and pensions. Every decision today is a step for tomorrow's freedom.

Now It's Up to You

Pay isn't just about money. It's about choice. Understanding the system means you don't just drift from job to job. You build towards a future on your terms.

Challenge 1: Step Up, Act with Purpose and Earn Your Pay

Don't wait for someone else to hand you an opportunity. Don't let payday simply 'happen' to you. Make it work for you today, tomorrow and in the long run.

You don't just want to get paid. You want to get paid well.

Payday isn't luck. It isn't guesswork. It's a result of knowing your worth, understanding the system and choosing to play the game with purpose.

You've got the process. You've got the strategy. Now it's about action.

Challenge 2: Don't Just Take What You're Given – Go Claim What You've Earned

The future doesn't reward those who drift along. It pays the ones who show up, step forward and act.

Ask the extra question, speak up when something doesn't look right, lean in rather than wait to be invited and your value will grow every time you choose to step forward instead of settling.

Opportunities rarely fall into your lap. Go create them by showing you're ready and willing.

Always remember to enjoy the journey – you never know where life will lead you. Don't worry if you take a wrong turn. Learn from it, correct the course and carry on. At the end of the day you'll find those wrong turnings were your life's greatest teachers.

And if you want to keep learning, stay curious or just follow along with more real-world payroll wisdom, I'd love to stay connected.

Keep In Touch

Email me on hayley@thepayrollguide.co.uk

Connect with me on LinkedIn. I post regular insights into payroll that you might find useful: www.linkedin.com/in/hayleypaterson

Are You a Payroll Professional in the Making?

If you've been reading along thinking, 'hang on…payroll sounds exciting', you're not wrong. It's fast-paced, full of variety and genuinely rewarding. There's always something new to learn and never a dull day.

Payroll isn't the 'easy option'. It will test you, teach you and grow you. You'll learn to think clearly under pressure, handle responsibility early and build skills that employers everywhere value.

Payroll is a career with rock-solid stability (people will always need to be paid), clear pathways to progress and skills that remain in demand for life. Every business relies on payroll, so you can work in any industry and build a future-proof career. Along the way you pick up skills that open doors everywhere – problem-solving, accuracy, communication, financial know-how and leadership. Skills that set you up for long-term success. Skills your friends and family will value in you. It's a profession with impact, purpose and plenty of room to grow. And it's one I absolutely love.

If it sparks your interest, explore it. If you want to talk it through, get in touch.

Jargon Buster: Your Payroll Vocabulary Toolkit

48-hour Rule
A rule under Working Time Regulations that says most workers shouldn't work more than an average of 48 hours per week (usually averaged over the previous 17 weeks), unless they choose to opt out.

Additional Voluntary Contribution (AVC)
Extra payments you choose to make into your pension on top of your normal contributions to boost your retirement savings.

Ad Hoc Worker
Someone brought in as needed for specific tasks or short periods.

Advisory, Conciliation and Arbitration Service (ACAS)
A government-funded organisation that provides free advice on workplace rights and helps resolve disputes between employers and employees.

Apprenticeship
A paid job where you learn while you work, combining real experience with training and qualifications.

Auto-enrolment
A system where eligible workers are automatically placed into a workplace pension scheme by their employer.

Average Hours
The average hours you work per week/day calculated over the last 52 weeks for holiday pay.

Average Weekly Earnings
What you typically earn per week, usually worked out using your last eight weeks' pay for Statutory Sick Pay.

Basic Pay
Your standard pay before any extras like overtime, bonuses or commission.

Benefit in Kind
Non-cash perks provided by your employer, such as a company car or private healthcare, which may still be taxable.

Bonus
An extra payment on top of your normal pay often given for good performance, meeting targets or at Christmas.

BR Tax Code
A tax code meaning all your income is taxed at the basic rate. Often used for second jobs.

Budget
A plan for how you'll spend and save your money that helps you stay in control of your finances.

Casual Worker
Someone who works occasionally or irregularly, often without guaranteed hours.

Clocking In and Out
Recording the time you start and finish work, often using a clocking in and out system or app.

Commission
Earnings based on sales or results. The more you sell or achieve the more you earn.

Company Handbook
A guide explaining workplace policies, rules and procedures. It is basically your employer's 'how things work here' manual.

Company Sick Pay
An employer's own sick pay scheme that pays more than Statutory Sick Pay (topping you up to full or partial pay).

Compound Interest
Interest calculated on your original money and the interest already added, meaning savings grow faster over time.

Continuing Professional Development (CPD)
Keeping your skills and knowledge up to date through ongoing learning. A requirement for certain professions.

Contract of Employment
A legal agreement between you and your employer that sets out your job role, pay, hours and workplace rights.

Credit Score
A rating that shows how reliable you are at borrowing and repaying money. Used by banks and lenders to decide whether to offer you credit.

Cumulative Basis
A method of calculating tax that looks at your total earnings and tax paid so far in the tax year to make sure you're paying the right amount overall.

Curriculum Vitae (CV)
A document that lists your skills, experience and qualifications to show employers why you're a good fit for a job.

D0 Tax Code
A tax code meaning all your income is taxed at the higher rate.

D1 Tax Code
A tax code meaning all your income is taxed at the additional rate.

Director
A person legally responsible for running a company and making key business decisions. Detailed on Companies House (the UK government's official register for limited companies).

Draw Your Pension
To start taking money from your pension savings when you reach retirement age.

Employee Contract
A legal agreement between you and your employer that sets out your job role, pay, hours and rights.

Employee Handbook
A guide provided by your employer that explains company rules, policies and how things operate at work.

Employee Number (Reference)
A unique reference number your employer gives you to identify you in their payroll system.

Employer Contributions
Payments your employer makes on top of your wages such as pension contributions or National Insurance.

ePayslip
An electronic version of your payslip that is usually accessed through an online portal or app.

Employer Payment Summary (EPS)
A report employers send to HMRC to claim reductions on what they owe. For example, for statutory payments, apprenticeship levy and employment allowance.

Fit Note
A doctor's note confirming you're not fit for work (or may be fit with adjustments) if you're off sick for more than seven days.

Fixed-term Contract
A contract that lasts for a set period or until a specific project ends.

Freelancing
A type of self-employment where you offer your skills to different clients often on short-term projects.

Full Payment Submission (FPS)
A report your employer sends to HMRC every time you're paid showing your earnings, tax and National Insurance details.

Future-proofing
Taking steps now to protect your finances and career against changes or challenges later in life.

General Data Protection Regulation (GDPR)
UK and EU laws that protect how organisations collect, store and use your personal data.

Glassdoor
A job and recruiting marketplace where employees share reviews of companies, salaries and interview experiences.

Gross Pay
Your total pay before tax, NI, pension contributions or any other deductions.

Gross vs Net
Gross pay is what you earn before deductions. Net pay is what lands in your bank account after tax and NI are taken off.

Hard Skills
Specific, teachable skills like using software, speaking a language or operating machinery.

His Majesty's Revenue & Customs (HMRC)
The government department responsible for collecting taxes and National Insurance in the UK.

Holiday Accrual
The process of building up holiday entitlement over time as you work.

Holiday Entitlement
The amount of paid leave you're legally allowed to take each year.

Holiday Pay
The pay you receive while taking annual leave. This is usually based on your normal earnings.

Hourly Paid
Being paid for each hour you work. Usually recorded on timesheets.

Income Tax
A tax taken from your earnings and paid to the government to fund public services.

Indeed
A popular job-search website that lists vacancies from employers across many industries.

Inflation
The gradual rise in prices over time meaning your money buys less than it used to.

Interest
The extra money you earn on savings or pay on borrowing.

Investment Returns
The profit (or loss) made from investments such as pensions or savings funds.

IR35
UK tax rules that decide whether a contractor is truly self-employed or should be taxed like an employee.

Job Advert
A listing posted by an employer describing an open job and how to apply.

Job Description
A document that explains what a job involves including duties, responsibilities and reporting lines.

Limited Company (Ltd)
The business is a separate legal entity from you. It offers more protection for personal assets but comes with more rules, reporting and admin.

Limited Liability Partnership (LLP)
Common for professional services. Partners run the business but their personal liability is limited.

LinkedIn
An online professional networking platform where you can build a profile, connect with employers and find job opportunities.

Lower Earnings Limit
The minimum level of earnings needed to count towards National Insurance qualifying years.

Marriage Allowance
A scheme that lets some married couples or civil partners transfer part of their tax-free allowance to their partner.

National Insurance (NI)
A system where workers in the UK contribute part of their earnings to fund things like the NHS, State Pension and certain benefits.

National Living Wage (NLW)
A higher legal minimum wage for workers aged 21 and over (set by the government).

National Minimum Wage (NMW)
The legal minimum hourly pay for workers in the UK, depending on your age.

Net Pay
The final amount you receive in your bank account after all deductions.

Next of Kin
The person your employer will contact in an emergency.

NIable Pay (Earnings for NI)
The proportion of your gross pay that is subject to NI.

NI Contributions

The employee and employer payments taken from your wages (or paid directly if you're a sole trader) to build your entitlement to state benefits.

NI Letter

A single letter which tells your employer how much NI to deduct and contribute for you.

NI Number

Your personal National Insurance number is a unique ID that tracks your NI contributions and tax records throughout your life.

Notice Period

The amount of time you or your employer must give before ending a job. Detailed in the contract of employment.

Overtime

Extra hours worked beyond your normal contracted hours. Usually paid at a higher rate.

P45

A form you get when you leave a job that shows how much you've earned and how much tax you've paid so far that year.

P60

A form given at the end of each tax year showing your total pay and tax paid. Useful for records or loan applications. Deadline is 31st May after the end of the tax year.

P800 Letter

A letter from HMRC telling you if you've paid too much or too little tax in a tax year.

Partnership
Two or more people run a business together and share profits, costs and responsibility. Each partner is usually personally liable.

Pay As You Earn (PAYE)
The system run by HMRC for calculating and collecting statutory deductions such as tax, NI and student loans.

Pay Frequency
How often you're paid. For example, weekly, fortnightly, four-weekly or monthly.

Pay Rise
An increase in your wages or salary often linked to performance, promotion or annual reviews.

Payroll
The process of calculating and paying employees correctly, including wages, tax, NI and pension deductions.

Payslip
A document (paper or digital) that shows your earnings, deductions and net pay each time you're paid.

Pension
A long-term savings plan designed to provide income when you retire.

Pension Contribution
Money saved for your retirement (often shown on the payslip as the pension provider's name).

Permanent Full-time Contract
A long-term contract where you work regular hours. Usually around 35–40 hours per week.

Permanent Part-time Contract
A long-term contract with fewer hours than full-time but with similar employment rights.

Person Specification
A list of the skills, experience and qualities an employer is looking for in a candidate.

Personal Tax Account (PTA)
Your online HMRC portal account where you can view and manage everything related to your tax in one place. Things like your tax code, National Insurance record, income history and any rebates or payments you're owed.

Prefix (Tax Code)
Letters at the start of a tax code that give HMRC and your employer information about your tax situation.

Primary Threshold
The earnings level at which employees start paying National Insurance contributions.

Pro Rata
A way of calculating pay or benefits in proportion to the time or hours worked. For example, part-time holiday entitlement.

Qualifying Years
Years in which you've paid enough National Insurance to count towards your State Pension entitlement.

Real Time Information (RTI)
A system where employers report pay, tax and National Insurance details to HMRC every time employees are paid.

Rolled-up Holiday Pay

A method where holiday pay is paid on top of your worked hours instead of being paid when you take leave.

Rolling 12-month Period

A moving year not a fixed January–December window. It looks back over the last 12 months at any point in time.

Rota

A work schedule showing when you're due to work.

Salary Paid

Being paid a fixed amount per year or month regardless of exact hours worked.

Secondary Threshold

The earnings level at which employers start paying National Insurance contributions for employees.

Self-assessment

A system where you report your own income to HMRC and pay any tax due. This is common for self-employed workers.

Self-certification

Telling your employer you're sick without a doctor's note. Allowed for up to seven calendar days.

Self-employed Contracts

An arrangement where you work for yourself and provide services to clients rather than being employed by a company.

Social Enterprise/Community Interest Company (CIC)

A business set up to benefit the community or a social cause with profits mainly reinvested rather than paid to owners.

Soft Skills
Personal skills like communication, teamwork and time management that help you work well with others.

Sole Trader
You run the business as an individual. It's simple to set up and run but you're personally responsible for any debts.

Starter Declaration
A statement you choose when starting a new job if you don't have a P45 from a previous employer, so your employer knows what tax code to set you up on.

State Pension
A regular payment from the government when you reach retirement age, based on your National Insurance record.

State Pension Age
The age at which you can start receiving the government State Pension.

Statutory
Rights that are protected by law. These apply to you no matter who your employer is and they're the foundation of fair work in the UK.

Statutory Adoption Pay (SAP)
Statutory pay provided to eligible employees when they take time off to adopt a baby.

Statutory Maternity Pay (SMP)
Statutory pay provided to eligible employees when they take time off to have a baby.

Statutory Paternity Pay (SPP)

Statutory pay provided to eligible employees taking time off when a child is born or adopted.

Statutory Payments

Minimum payments set by law that employers must provide in certain situations such as sick pay, maternity pay or paternity pay.

Statutory Sick Pay (SSP)

The minimum sick pay employers must provide if you're off work due to illness and meet eligibility rules.

Student Loan

Money borrowed to pay for education which you repay automatically from your wages once you earn above a certain amount (dependent on your loan type).

Suffix (Tax Code)

Letters at the end of a tax code that signal special tax circumstances such as adjustments to allowances.

Taxable Pay (Earnings for Tax)

The part of your pay that tax is calculated on after any tax-free allowances are applied.

Tax Code

A code of (sometimes) a prefix, numbers and suffix which tells your employer how much tax to deduct.

Tax Relief

A reduction in tax often given on pension contributions or certain expenses.

TD

To-date totals for the current tax year (starting 6th April).

Upper Earnings Limit
The point at which the rate of National Insurance contributions changes on higher earnings.

Union
An organisation that represents workers, offering support, advice and protection at work.

Working Time Regulations
UK laws that set rules on working hours, breaks and paid holiday to protect workers.

Year to Date (YTD)
A running total from the start of the tax year up to your most recent payslip.

Zero-hour Contract
A contract where the employer doesn't guarantee any hours and you work only when offered shifts.

Links

Below are a few links to websites I've discussed within the book or that you might find handy.

Note: These links worked at the time of writing. As information and resources are updated all the time, they may not work at the time of reading.

ACAS:
https://www.acas.org.uk

GDPR guidance:
https://www.gov.uk/personal-data-my-employer-can-keep-about-me

HMRC:
https://www.gov.uk

HMRC Tax Calculator:
https://www.gov.uk/estimate-income-tax

Holiday Pay Guidance:
https://www.gov.uk/holiday-entitlement-rights

IR35 (Off-payroll Working):
https://www.gov.uk/guidance/understanding-off-payroll-working-ir35

Personal Tax Account (PTA) Set Up:
https://www.gov.uk/personal-tax-account

School-leaver Age for Holiday Entitlement:
https://www.gov.uk/know-when-you-can-leave-school

Student Loan Guidance:
https://www.gov.uk/guidance/special-rules-for-student-loans

Working Time Regulations:
https://www.acas.org.uk/working-time-rules

About Hayley Paterson

Hayley Paterson is the person behind The Payroll Guide Ltd and Chanonry Payroll Solutions Ltd, but before the job titles and businesses she was once exactly where you are now – starting out, figuring things out and learning how the world of work really works.

Hayley has spent over 23 years working in payroll, beginning her career in 2003 and learning the ropes across different industries including oil and gas, and within payroll bureaux, working with businesses of all shapes and sizes. Over the years she's worked on payrolls for one employee and for workforces of more than 8,000, which means she's seen just about every question, mistake and 'why didn't anyone tell me this?' moment there is.

In late 2017 as she prepared to return to work after having her son, Hayley founded Chanonry Payroll Solutions Ltd. What started as one business soon grew into two clear paths – outsourced payroll services and payroll consulting. In 2025 she split the business, creating The Payroll Guide – a brand focused on helping people and businesses understand payroll clearly, confidently and without the jargon.

Hayley lives on the Black Isle in the Scottish Highlands with her husband Michael, their son Alfie and their dog Misty. Surrounded by big skies and coastal views she's a firm believer that every career is a journey and that there's no single right route, just informed choices along the way.

Pay Me, Hayley's second book, was written because Hayley knows how confusing payslips, contracts and workplace rights can feel when no one explains them properly. This book exists to be the guide she wishes she'd had at the start – practical, honest and on your side as you take the steering wheel and begin your own journey into the world of work.

Hayley doesn't just love payroll, she lives it. She's passionate about helping employers, like the ones you'll work for, unlock the hidden potential within their payroll processes, showing them that payroll doesn't have to be a source of stress and confusion that it often is for employers. This is why she wrote her first book *The Value of Payroll*. With her guidance, employers can streamline their payroll operations and focus on what really matters – growing their business and looking after their employees, safe in the knowledge that they have their payroll process firmly under control.

Hayley's mission is simple: to provide meaningful communication that transforms how people experience payroll. To make payroll easier for you, your employer and to be a trusted guide through the employment journey.

www.ingramcontent.com/pod-product-compliance
Lightning Source LLC
LaVergne TN
LVHW022208200926
848481LV00006B/1887